ADOBE PHOTOSHOP 2024

USER GUIDE

THE COMPLETE STEP-BY-STEP BEGINNER TO EXPERT ILLUSTRATIVE GUIDE TO MASTERING ADOBE PHOTOSHOP 2024 WITH UPDATED SHORTCUTS, TIPS & TRICKS

PETER JOHN

TABLE OF CONTENT

INTRODUCTION .... **VIII**

CHAPTER ONE **1**

ADOBE PHOTOSHOP`S FEATURE OVERVIEW **1**

NEW FEATURES IN PHOTOSHOP 2024 2

THE MINIMUM AND RECOMMENDED REQUIREMENTS OF PHOTOSHOP 2024 4

DOWNLOADING & INSTALLING PHOTOSHOP 2024 7

DOWNLOADING PHOTOSHOP 2024 7

INSTALLING PHOTOSHOP 2024 8

CHAPTER TWO **12**

GETTING TO KNOW THE WORKSPACE **12**

WORKING WITH THE HOME SCREEN 12

PHOTOSHOP WORKSPACES 15

WORKING WITH THE WORKSPACE 18

THE CONTEXTUAL TASKBAR 21

WORKING WITH THE MENU BAR 22

PHOTOSHOP`S TOOL BAR 39

AN OVERVIEW OF PHOTOSHOP TOOLS 41

MANAGING WINDOWS AND PANELS 55

CHAPTER THREE **58**

BASIC CONCEPTS & PRACTICAL TUTORIALS IN PHOTOSHOP **58**

WORKING WITH DOCUMENTS/PROJECTS 58

CREATING A NEW DOCUMENT 58

USING THE OPEN RECENT COMMAND 61

INSERTING IMAGES VIA DRAG & DROP 62

IMPORTING IMAGES FROM LIGHTROOM 62

INSERTING IMAGES/FILES IN EXISTING DOCUMENTS 63

INSERTING FILES VIA PLACE EMBEDDED 63

INSERTING FILES VIA PLACE-LINKED 64

PLACE EMBEDDED VS PLACE LINKED 66

WORKING WITH SMART OBJECTS 68

EXPORTING FILES OUT OF PHOTOSHOP 69

CHAPTER FOUR **74**

DIGITAL IMAGES AND COLOR MODES IN PHOTOSHOP **74**

HAVING SUFFICIENT KNOWLEDGE OF DIGITAL IMAGES 74

PRACTICAL APPLICATIONS.. 75
UNDERSTANDING COLOR MODES.. **76**
RGB COLOR MODE 77
CMYK COLOR MODE... 77
LAB COLOR MODE 78
INDEXED COLOR MODE 78
GRAYSCALE COLOR MODE 78
BITMAP COLOR MODE 79
DUOTONE COLOR MODE 79
MULTICHANNEL COLOR MODE... 79

CHAPTER FIVE 81

LAYERS; ONE OF THE FINEST TOOLS IN PHOTOSHOP 81

UNDERSTANDING LAYERS.. **81**
LAYER BASICS **83**
WORKING WITH LAYERS... **88**
WORKING WITH ADJUSTMENTS LAYERS **94**
ADJUSTMENT PRESETS... 97
ADJUSTMENT LAYERS... 98
THE THREE AUTO-COMMANDS.. **122**
BEHIND THE SCENE- HOW THE AUTO CONTRAST, AUTO TONE, AND AUTO COLOR OPERATE 123
AUTO CONTRAST... 125
AUTO TONE 126
AUTO COLOR 126
BLENDING MODES IN PHOTOSHOP **127**
UNDERSTANDING EACH BLENDING MODE FOR THEIR UNIQUENESS.. 129
NORMAL BLENDING MODES.. 129
DARKEN BLENDING MODES... 130
LIGHTEN BLENDING MODES 131
CONTRAST BLENDING MODES 132
INVERSION BLENDING MODES... 134
COMPONENT BLENDING MODES.. 135
SPICING UP YOUR DESIGNS WITH LAYER STYLES... **136**
PRESET STYLES.. 138
LAYER EFFECTS 140

CHAPTER SIX 144

SELECTING AND MASKING 144

STARTING WITH SELECTION AND SELECTION TOOLS **144**
THE MARQUEE TOOLS... 145
THE LASSO TOOLS 146
OBJECT SELECTION TOOLS 148

SELECT OBJECT 150
SELECT SKY 150
COLOR RANGE 151
FOCUS AREA 156
USING THE QUICK MASK MODE 158
SELECTING AND MASKING 161
THE SELECT AND MASK OPTIONS 161
REFINE THE SELECTION 167

CHAPTER SEVEN 172

TYPOGRAPHY; THE TYPE TOOLS IN PHOTOSHOP 172

THE BASICS OF TYPOGRAPHY 172
USING TEXTS IN PHOTOSHOP 176
THE CHARACTER PANEL AND THE PARAGRAPH PANEL 176
WORKING WITH TEXTS.. 185

CHAPTER EIGHT 191

TRANSFORMING IMAGES IN PHOTOSHOP 191

INTRODUCTION TO THE TRANSFORM TOOL IN PHOTOSHOP 191
OTHER TRANSFORM OPTIONS IN PHOTOSHOP 191
FREE TRANSFORM.. 193
TRANSFORM.. 197
CONTENT-AWARE: GENERATIVE FILL, CONTENT-AWARE FILL, AND CONTENT-AWARE SCALE 197
USING AI GENERATIVE FILL 198
CONTENT-AWARE FILL 201
CONTENT-AWARE SCALE.. 203
HOW TO PROTECT AN OBJECT WHILE USING THE CONTENT-AWARE SCALE 205
THE CROP TOOL AND ITS OTHER RELATED TOOLS... 205
THE CROP TOOL.. 205
PERSPECTIVE CROP TOOL.. 208
THE SLICE TOOL 209
THE SELECT SLICE TOOL.. 211

CHAPTER NINE 215

RETOUCHING TOOLS IN PHOTOSHOP.. 215

IMAGE RETOUCHING IN PHOTOSHOP 215
RETOUCHING TOOLS IN PHOTOSHOP 216
THE SPOT HEALING BRUSH 216
THE HEALING BRUSH.. 219
THE PATCH TOOL... 222
CONTENT-AWARE MOVE TOOL 224

RED EYE TOOL 227
CLONE STAMP TOOL 229
PATTERN STAMP BRUSH 231
THE BLUR TOOL, SHARPEN TOOL AND SMUDGE TOOL 233
THE BLUR TOOL 233
THE SHARPEN TOOL 235
THE SMUDGE TOOL 237
THE DODGE TOOL, BURN TOOL, AND SPONGE TOOL 240
THE DODGE TOOL 241
THE BURN TOOL 244
THE SPONGE TOOL 246
OTHER RETOUCHING TOOLS IN PHOTOSHOP – BRUSH TOOLS 250
THE BRUSH TOOL 250
THE PEN TOOL 255
COLOR REPLACEMENT TOOL 259
MIXER BRUSH TOOL 264
HISTORY BRUSH TOOL 269
THE HISTORY PANEL IN PHOTOSHOP 269
USING THE HISTORY BRUSH TOOL 270
THE ART HISTORY BRUSH TOOL 272
WORKING WITH THE ERASER TOOL 275

CHAPTER TEN 282

FILTERS IN PHOTOSHOP 282

INTRODUCTION TO PHOTOSHOP FILTERS 282
KNOWING HOW TO USE FILTERS IN PHOTOSHOP 284
EXTENDED FILTERS 284
USING THE NEURAL FILTERS 285
FILTER GALLERY 287
ADAPTIVE WIDE ANGLE 288
CAMERA RAW FILTER 288
LENS CORRECTION 289
LIQUIFY 290
VANISHING POINT 291
ARTISTIC FILTER 292
BLUR FILTERS 293
BLUR GALLERY FILTERS 295
BRUSH STROKES FILTERS 295
DISTORT FILTERS 296
NOISE FILTERS 297
PIXELATE FILTERS 297
RENDER FILTERS 298
STYLIZE FILTERS 299

SHARPEN FILTERS..300
VIDEO FILTERS...301
OTHER FILTERS...302

CHAPTER ELEVEN 303

TIPS AND TRICKS ON PHOTOSHOP 2024............................303

TIPS AND TRICKS.. 303
THE PREFERENCE WINDOW 303
PREFERENCE TO IMPROVE SELECTION STABILITY 306
SHORTCUTS FOR BLENDING MODES..306
SAVING SELECTIONS IN PHOTOSHOP..308
LOADING SELECTIONS IN PHOTOSHOP...309
POPULAR SHORTCUTS IN PHOTOSHOP..310
FUNCTION KEYS SHORTCUTS 311
SHORTCUTS FOR SELECTION TOOLS..312
SHORTCUTS FOR VIEWING IMAGES 314
SHORTCUT FOR SELECTING AND MOVING OBJECTS.........................315
SHORTCUTS FOR SELECTING AND EDITING TEXTS...........................316

TROUBLESHOOTING IN PHOTOSHOP 317
USING THE SELECT SUBJECT OR OBJECT SELECTION TOOL CAUSES [WIN] TO CRASH. 318
WHEN OPENING NEW DOCUMENTS, A GREEN SCREEN ISSUE OCCURS..318
NOT RECOGNIZING THE PICTURE SIZE COPIED TO THE CLIPBOARD 318
PHOTOSHOP LAUNCHES SLOWLY 319
PHOTOSHOP WON'T ACCEPT DESKTOP PHOTOS FROM LIGHTROOM...320
PHOTOSHOP UNABLE TO EXPLORE IN BRIDGE 320

CONCLUSION 321

INTRODUCTION

Adobe Photoshop 2024 User Guide is here. This book aims to teach you everything there is to know about the most widely used image editing programs worldwide. This book will help you become an expert Photoshop user and produce amazing images, covering everything from the fundamentals to more complex techniques.

A powerful tool that can be used for many different tasks is Adobe Photoshop. These tasks include photography, digital arts, graphic design, video editing, etc.

Photoshop can be used for a multitude of photo editing tasks, including cropping, resizing, adjusting brightness and colors, and eliminating blemishes.

Photoshop can be used for graphic design, which includes making graphics for print, social media, and websites.

Photoshop is a tool that can be used to produce concept art, paintings, and drawings.

Regardless of your degree of experience, there is something for you to learn from this book. You will learn the fundamentals of image editing, including how to use layers, masks, and filters, if you are a beginner. You will learn advanced techniques like color correction, compositing, and photo manipulation if you are an experienced user.

CHAPTER ONE

ADOBE PHOTOSHOP`S FEATURE OVERVIEW

The Adobe Photoshop software application was developed by Adobe Inc. and made available for Windows and macOS. Photoshop was developed in 1987 by the American brothers Thomas and John Knoll, and in 1988 they sold the distribution rights to Adobe Inc. Since then, the program has developed into the industry standard for all types of digital art, including manipulating raster graphics.

The fact that Photoshop has changed over the years—from version 0.07 to Photoshop CS, Photoshop CC, and finally to Photoshop 2024 (Version 25.0)—is undisputed.

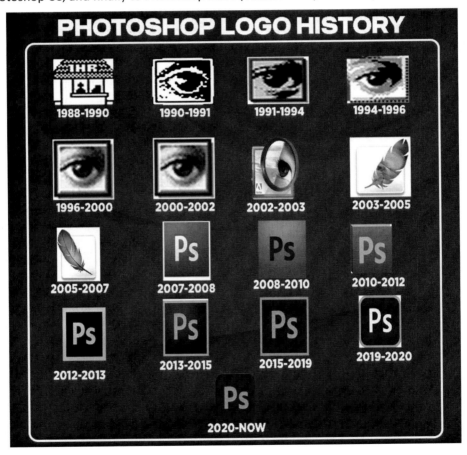

- The New Features available in Photoshop 2024
- The Minimum and Recommended system requirements for Photoshop 2024
- Downloading and installation of Photoshop 2024

New Features in Photoshop 2024

- **Generative Fill and Generative Expand available in Photoshop:** These new generative AI technologies, powered by ***Adobe FireFly*** (An Adobe AI built into Creative Cloud to enable users to swiftly generate results and then modify them to meet their unique vision.), allow you to add, remove, or expand content from images non-destructively, in seconds, using simple text prompts within the app in over 100 languages to achieve realistic results that will surprise, delight, and astound you.

They instantaneously adjust to your image's perspective, lighting, and style to achieve stunning effects. Your newly generated information is created in a Generative layer, where you may apply Photoshop's power and precision to improve your image beyond your expectations.

- **Contextual Task Bar Updated**: To assist you in moving forward with your masking and generative AI workflows, additional enhancements to the Contextual Task.

✦ **Remove Tool Updated**: With the Remove tool's new interactivity, all you have to do to remove an area from an image is to build a loop (circle) around it rather than just brushing past it. You don't need to close the loop because Photoshop will figure out the distance and eliminate distractions for you. Time can be saved and brushing errors are decreased as a result.
If you accidentally pick something while enclosing an area, switch the brush stroke mode from addition to subtraction in the settings bar to fix it.

✦ **Parametric Filters (Beta)**: Similar to how neural filters were brought to Photoshop in 2023, parametric filters have also been included in Photoshop 25.1 but are only available in the Beta version. The Parametric filters include several different effects, such as duotone, color, chromatic effect, and black and white.

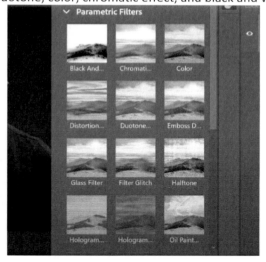

- **Adjustment Presets**: Adjustment Presets are among the most recent features added to Photoshop, as you will see if you contrast Photoshop v25 with its earlier iterations. Adobe has pre-made effects called Adjustment Presets that are designed to enhance the Photoshop experience for users.

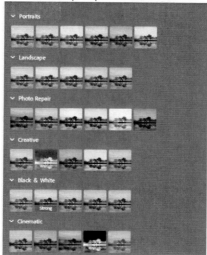

- **Other improvements and modifications include**:
  - Improve startup performance by initializing views on demand.
  - support for new lenses and cameras.
  - Unable to sync presets.

The Minimum and Recommended Requirements of Photoshop 2024

Before downloading and installing Adobe Photoshop 2024 on your computer, you should first check to see if it can run on your Windows or Mac system. Another reason you should know in advance if your Windows and Mac can use this software is because it now has a few updated and sophisticated features.

To run and utilize Photoshop, your computer must fulfill the minimal requirements listed below.

For Windows

	Minimum	Recommended
Processor	2 GHz or faster multicore Intel® or AMD processor with SSE 4.2 or later and 64-bit support	

Operating system	Preferably Windows 10 64-bit (version 22H2); Versions of LTSC are not supported.	
RAM	8 GB	16 GB or more
Graphics card	• DirectX 12 (feature level 12_0 or later)-capable GPU • GPUs that are less than 7 years old, with 1.5 GB of memory (upgrade display drivers from the GPU manufacturer's website). Testing on GPUs older than seven years is not supported.	• GPU that supports DirectX 12 at feature level 12_0 or above. • 4 GB of GPU memory or more for 4K displays
Monitor resolution	Displaying at 100% UI scaling in 1280 by 800	minimum 1920 x 1080 display at 100% UI scaling
Hard disk space	20 GB of available hard disk space	100 GB of available hard disk space • Fast internal SSD for app installation • Separate internal drive for scratch disks
Internet	Access to online services, subscription verification, and essential program activation require internet connection and registration.	
Processor	ARM processor	
Operating system	Windows 10 ARM device running Windows 10 64-bit (version 20H2) or later	

5

RAM	8 GB	16 GB or more
Graphics card	4 GB of GPU memory	
Every other specification for ARM also applies to INTEL		

For macOS

	Minimum	Recommended
Processor	2 GHz or faster multicore Intel® or Apple Silicon CPU with SSE 4.2 or later and 64-bit support	ARM-based Apple Silicon processor
Operating system	macOS Big Sur (version 11.0) or later	Ventura (version 13.4) of macOS V10.15.x installations are prohibited.
RAM	8 GB	16 GB or more
Graphics card	• GPU with Metal support • 1.5 GB of GPU memory	• Metal-supporting GPU • 4 GB of GPU memory or more for 4K displays
Monitor resolution	Displaying at 100% UI scaling in 1280 by 800	Minimum 1920 x 1080 display at 100% UI scaling
Hard disk space	20 GB of available hard disk space	100 GB of available hard disk space • Fast internal SSD for app installation • Additional high-speed drive(s) or SSD to set up scratch disk

	Installing Photoshop won't work on a volume with a case-sensitive file system.
Internet	Access to online services, membership verification, and essential software activation require internet connection and registration.
Processor	ARM-based Apple Silicon processor
Operating system	macOS Big Sur (version 11.2.2) or later	
RAM	8 GB	16 GB or more

Downloading & Installing Photoshop 2024

Downloading Photoshop 2024

Follow the instructions below to successfully download Photoshop 2024

- ✦ On your web browser, enter the URL link below to download Photoshop 2024:
  https://filecr.com/windows/adobe-photoshop-2023-0061/?id=643703320000
- ✦ Carefully read through the instructions that are present on the website page
- ✦ Click on **Direct Download**.

- ✦ You will be opened up to a new tab, click on **Download** to download Photoshop 2024 Setup on your PC.

Thanks for Downloading

Adobe Photoshop

⬇ **Click to Download**

The password for Zip file is: 123

For more help please visit Faqs

Installing Photoshop 2024

After you have successfully downloaded Photoshop 2024, follow the procedures below to install it on your PC.

✦ Extract the Photoshop software application from its encoded file format using WINRAR and extract it to the desired location of your choice on your PC.

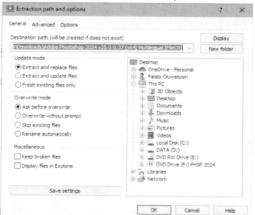

✦ Open the extracted folder, open the **DISC file**

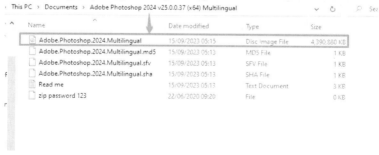

✦ Open a folder named "**Adobe 2024**".

8

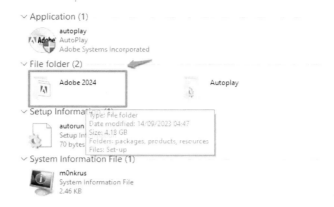

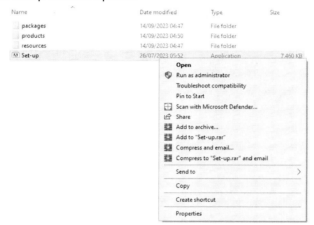

✦ Select the Setup File and open it.

✦ Follow the instructions displayed on your screen to the end to successfully install Photoshop 2024 on your PC.

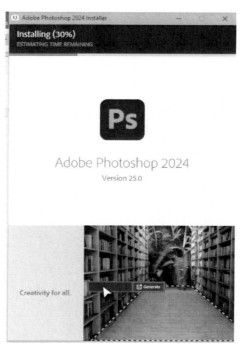

After installing Photoshop on your PC. Launch it and a preview will appear on your screen like the one below. This means that Photoshop has been successfully installed and running.

CHAPTER TWO

GETTING TO KNOW THE WORKSPACE

What you will learn in this chapter.

- **How to maximize the home screen and the several workspaces available in Photoshop.**
- **Working with the Menu Bar**
- **Selecting and using the tools available in Photoshop**
- **Opening the panel docks and using a panel effectively.**

Working With the Home Screen

The Home Screen is the first thing to see on the interface when Photoshop is launched. Your Home Screen layout is customized according to your Creative Cloud subscription plan and your experience with Photoshop. Because you haven't done any work on your home screen yet, it will appear empty; over time, your most recent creations will start to surface there. Click the Home icon in the Options bar to return to the home screen at any time while editing a Photoshop document. Simply press the Esc key to leave the home screen.

The Home screen, which appears when Photoshop is launched, contains the following:

⇕ **Photoshop Logo**: It is located right below the Menu Panel. The logo, when clicked, a default Workspace is displayed.

⇕ **Menu Panel**: The Menu panel is located in the upper-left corner of the home screen and contains the following options: File, Edit, Image, Layer, Type, Select, Filter, 3D, View, Plugins, Window, and Help. When using Photoshop, you may quickly and freely access all of these.

- A variety of tutorials to aid in your quick learning and comprehension of the ideas, procedures, and concepts available in Photoshop, including helpful hints.

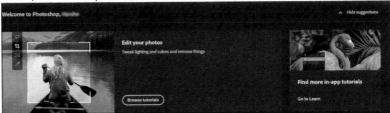

- Documents you've recently accessed or shared with you in the cloud will be shown and accessible under **Recents** on your home screen. Additionally, you can use a keyword to filter cloud documents. When offline, you can still use a keyword to filter cloud documents, but those that are only accessible online will have a grayed-out appearance.

- **New File**: When starting a new document for a project, you click on this button. As seen below.

- **Open**: You can open files from your computer's storage or cloud storage by clicking on this button.
- **Home**: To access the Home screen, click this tab.

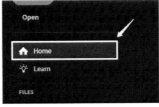

◆ **Learn**: To get started with Photoshop, click this tab to view a range of beginner's and expert tutorials.

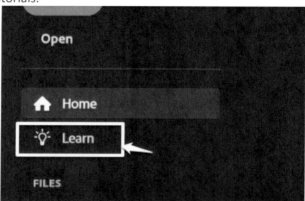

◆ **Files**: There are four parts in this area of the home screen. **Your Files, Shared With You, Lightroom Photos**, and **Deleted**. Without first logging into Cloud Creative, you cannot access this section.

- ◆ The files that are synced with your creative cloud storage are referred to as "**Your Files.**"
- ◆ **Shared With You**: These are files that coworkers, designers, etc. have given you access to.
- ◆ **Lightroom Photos**: This allows you to access and import synched images from Adobe Lightroom.
- ◆ **Deleted**: This section contains files that you have deleted from your creative cloud. This is Photoshop's recycling bin option.

Photoshop Workspaces

Various components, including panels, bars, and windows, are used when creating and manipulating an image, data, and projects. A workspace can be any setup of these components. Photoshop may be customized to fit the way you work by choosing from several preset workspaces or by building your own. The workspace refers to Photoshop's user interface.

A workspace displays on your screen by default, when you create a new file or open an existing file.

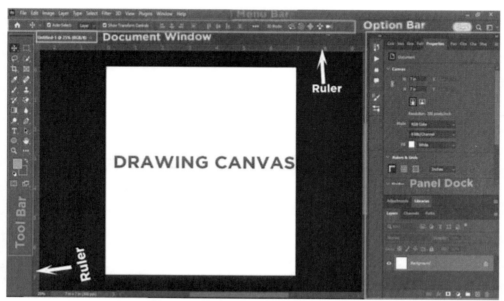

The workspace in Photoshop is made up of the following main components:

- **Drawing Canvas**: It serves as the canvas board upon which your projects and images are displayed. Below is a drawing canvas displaying a project.

♣ **Menu Bar**: Located at the top of the workspace, it contains doors that lead to some important features/commands on Photoshop. These doors are **File**, **Edit**, **Image**, **Layer**, **Type**, **Select**, **Filter**, **3D**, **Plugins**, **View**, **Window**, and **Help.**

These doors further contain submenus for relevant items. *For instance,* ***Windows*** *allows you to change your workspace and its contents.*

♣ **Tool Panel**: There are tools for producing and altering pictures, artwork, page elements, and other things in the Tools section. This panel is located on the left side of your workspace.

16

There is a grouping of related tools. *For instance, the Move Tool and the Artboard Tool are grouped in the Move Tool. Right-click your mouse to access the contents of a grouped tool.*

✦ **Option Bar**: Options (other controls) for the presently selected tool are shown in the Options bar. It is located right below the Menu Bar. *The image below is the option bar for the Brush Tool.*

✦ **Panels**: You can track and edit your work with the help of the Panels. *Below is the Properties Panel.*

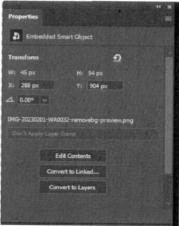

Panels may be docked, stacked, or clustered together.

✦ **Rulers**: When trying to find precise distances between two spots to correct photographs, the Ruler tool is extremely useful. Use Ctrl/Command + R to display your rulers.

Working with The Workspace

The Essentials is the default workspace in Photoshop because it is a multipurpose workspace, it is a basic workspace that is typically thought to be more practical and useful.

In Photoshop, we may organize the Photoshop toolbar and determine which panels will be displayed in our workspace. Workspaces have configurable menus and keyboard shortcuts as well. We can quickly adapt the Photoshop layout to our preferred working style and certain activities. There are many panels available in Photoshop, including the brush, channels, layers, masks, etc.

Photoshop includes several workspaces by default, including those for **3D**, **design**, **motion**, **painting**, **graphics**, and **photography**, among others. Because Photoshop has so many panels, it is not a good idea to display them all in your workspace. To select the workspace you desire,

✦ Select the **Window** Menu and click **Workspace**
✦ From the Workspace Menu, Pick the desired workspace of your choice. **Essential** is a good workspace for beginners.

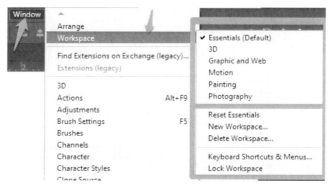

You can arrange the panels that appear in your workspace and choose how the toolbar is presented. The menus and keyboard shortcuts in workspaces can be customized. The Photoshop layout can be rapidly modified to fit your chosen working method and certain tasks. The brush, channels, layers, masks, and other panels are only a few of the many panels that Photoshop offers.

To add a panel to your workspace, follow the procedure below,

18

- Select **Windows** in the **Menu bar**
- A series of panels are displayed, Pick the panel of your choice and it displays automatically on your screen.
- You can either add your panes to your **Panel Dock** or anywhere you desire.

Do the following to reset your workspace.

- Select **Windows** in the **Menu bar** and select **Workspace** from the drop-down menu.

- Select **Reset Essentials** from the drop-down menu.

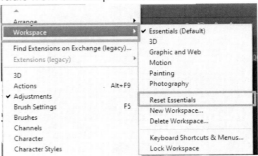

Do the following to create a new Workspace.

- Be sure your panels, toolbar, and other tabs are arranged the way you need them to be.
- Select **Windows** in the **Menu bar** and select **Workspace** from the drop-down menu.

- Select **New Workspace** from the drop-down menu.

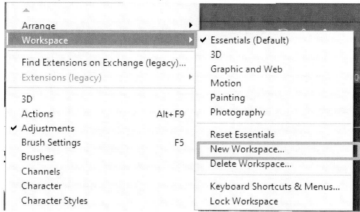

- Name your new workspace and select Save.

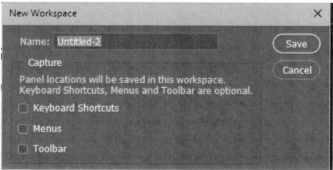

Do the following to delete a workspace.

- Make sure that the workspace you desire to delete is not currently opened.
- Select **Windows** in the **Menu bar** and select **Workspace** from the drop-down menu.

♦ Select **Delete Workspace** from the drop-down menu.

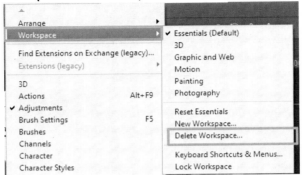

♦ From the menu preview that pops up on the screen, select the workspace you want to delete and click on **Delete**.

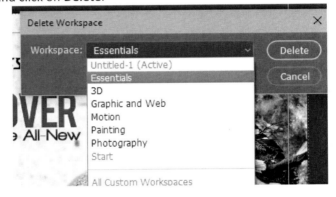

The Contextual Taskbar

The contextual taskbar Quick Command taskbar appears on your workspace when you launch your Photoshop. It contains some quick commands such as *Select Subject* and *Remove Background*.

Click on the three dots at the right side of the bar to edit your taskbar.

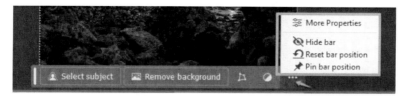

- Selecting *More Properties* takes you to the *Properties Panel*
- *Hide bar* hides the contextual taskbar
- **Reset bar position** allows you to change the position of the taskbar.
- *Pin bar position* allows you to pin the taskbar on a fixed position.

Working with The Menu Bar

One of the core elements of Adobe Photoshop is the menu bar, which is located at the top of the program. The menu bar is used to launch and close windows, modify the size of the canvas, access some editing tools, open and save files, and more.

File, **Edit**, **Image**, **Layer**, **Type**, **Select**, **Filter**, **3D**, **View**, **Plugins**, **Window**, and **Help** are the 12 options in the menu bar. There are further submenus for relevant items under each of those primary menus. The majority of the items on the menu bar can also be accessed through keyboard shortcuts, right-click menus, or specific menus found inside other windows like Tools, Layers, Timeline, etc. However, for some settings, you must use the menu bar. Let`s do a quick review of each of the following options in the menu bar.

File: Photoshop's File menu is very similar to the File menu in other applications. It serves as the main tool for creating new files, opening them, saving them, and printing them.

22

For instance, you can utilize the File menu to pick **Open** to explore the image you want to use if you've just opened Photoshop and want to import a PNG or JPG file. Additionally, advanced open actions including Opening Smart Objects, saving photographs for web use to reduce the size, and exporting to a video format are enabled. The 10 most recently opened files are listed under the **Open Recent** option under the File menu. You can utilize that option to quickly re-open a file without going through the typical "open, select, browse" process, provided you haven't relocated the original file somewhere else.

The File menu is where you may also convert a video.

Edit: You can change menu items, shortcuts, objects on the canvas, and more with the Edit menu.

You can, for instance, cut, copy, and paste as well as simply undo or redo a recent activity. You'll use those menu selections frequently or at the very least become familiar with their keyboard shortcuts because those are frequent actions.

Undo Quick Selection	Ctrl+Z
Redo	Shift+Ctrl+Z
Toggle Last State	Alt+Ctrl+Z
Fade...	Shift+Ctrl+F
Cut	Ctrl+X
Copy	Ctrl+C
Copy Merged	Shift+Ctrl+C
Paste	Ctrl+V
Paste Special	▸
Clear	

You may work with text and selections via the Edit menu, where you can search for and replace certain words and phrases throughout a document. Additionally, you can choose to **Fill selections** or Add a **Stroke** along a chosen path.

There are also tools for object transformation here. Use the **Edit** > **Transform submenu** to find the options if you wish to warp, rotate, scale, distort, or flip an image. You may also find the Free Transform tool in this area, which allows you to change the height, breadth, and orientation.

To see brushes, gradients, swatches, and custom shapes, and load your custom ABR brushes, launch Preset Manager from the Edit menu.

To modify RGB, CMYK, and other color profiles, you can also open Color Settings (and also load custom CSF and PSP files). The Sky replacement feature, content-aware scale, and many others are also accessible in the Edit menu.

This menu is used to find already-existing keyboard shortcuts, define new ones, modify general Photoshop preferences, and show/hide which items are displayed on the menu bar.

Keyboard Shortcuts...	Alt+Shift+Ctrl+K
Menus...	Alt+Shift+Ctrl+M
Toolbar...	
Preferences	

Image: Under the Image menu in Photoshop, there are a lot of choices for altering photos.

You can switch the mode of the entire canvas using the first submenu; **Mode.** You can choose from modes like RGB color, grayscale, CMYK color, multichannel, duotone, and more.

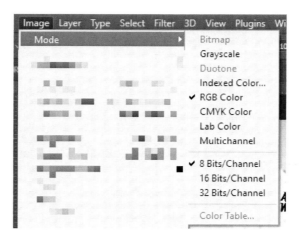

The **Adjustments** submenu is the next, and it provides access to several tools for adjusting an image's brightness, contrast, levels, exposure, Vibrance, hue/saturation, and color balance. The tools for the Photo Filter, Channel Mixer, and Color Lookup are all included here as well.

With the Auto Tone, Auto Contrast, and Auto Color choices, adjustments can be made to an image's appearance without using menus or sliders.

Auto Tone	Shift+Ctrl+L
Auto Contrast	Alt+Shift+Ctrl+L
Auto Color	Shift+Ctrl+B

The Image menu's **Image Size** and **Canvas Size** options are useful tools for manipulating Canvas. To make the entire working area the precise size that it needs to be or to downsize or increase the canvas, you would use the Canvas Size option. **Image Rotation** in the image menu allows for the rotation of images.

Other noteworthy tools on this menu are **Crop** and **Trim**. At first, the canvas is resized by manually choosing which regions should be eliminated. The second option automates resizing by erasing translucent or predetermined-color pixels from any canvas edge.

Image Size...	Alt+Ctrl+I
Canvas Size...	Alt+Ctrl+C
Image Rotation	▶
Crop	
Trim...	
Reveal All	

Layer: You can add new layers, duplicate existing ones, and delete and rename layers, among other things, via the Layer menu.

Options for adding layer masks, adjustment layers, and fill layers are also included in this menu. For instance, when you click on a fill layer, a new layer is created that is already filled with the color, pattern, or gradient of your choice.

Additionally, you can create and edit Smart Objects using the Layer menu, as well as export or replace their contents with those of other Smart Objects.

You can also link and merge layers, group and hide layers, lock layers, place layers in front of or behind other layers, flatten the image to automatically merge all the layers, and group and hide layers using other choices in the Layer menu.

Type: The first option under "Type" in Adobe Photoshop is "Panels." The fly-out menu for this option reveals several sets of possibilities. These are:

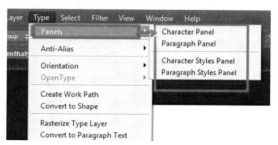

✦ Character Panel is like an extended version of the options bar after you select the type tool.

- Paragraph Panels: this is like an extension of the alignment panel for the type tool.
- The next option in the Type Menu is **Anti-Alias**, this option is utilized to make the letter edges appear smooth. The majority of the letters will "appear blocky" and "hard-edged" if this option is not selected.
- The text can position itself "horizontally" and "vertically" with the following option, **Orientation**.
- **Create Work Path** converts texts to a path, **Convert to Shape** changes a text to a shape, **Rasterize Type layer** converts a layer type to a raster image,
- **Convert to Point text** converts texts to character type
- **Warp Text** allows you to twist your texts into any form
- **Match Fonts** searches your desktop fonts library and creative cloud storage to show you type fonts that are similar to the one you have selected in a design.
- **Font preview** allows you to decide how your fonts will be displayed when you type text. You can discover the other features in the type menu by exploring them too.

Select: The Select menu in Photoshop contains options related to selections.

From this menu, you can pick or deselect every item on the canvas as well as every layer. You can re-select a previous selection and invert the selection using a few relevant and practical tools.

All	Ctrl+A
Deselect	Ctrl+D
Reselect	Shift+Ctrl+D
Inverse	Shift+Ctrl+I
All Layers	Alt+Ctrl+A
Deselect Layers	
Find Layers	Alt+Shift+Ctrl+F
Isolate Layers	

Advanced selection options like color range, focus area, subject, and sky are accessible in the select menu

The Select menu contains the **Select and Mask** tool which contains a Refine Edge tool that you can use to alter a selection's edge. Specific selection details can be defined by adjusting the smooth, feather, contrast, and shift edge parameters.

Modify allows you to make changes to the size of your selection.

To efficiently expand the selection area, **Grow** automatically expands a selection to surrounding pixels. If you click it repeatedly, more options will appear.

To re-select something later, use Save Selection and Load Selection. When you need to apply a new selection again, you can save it and then load it.

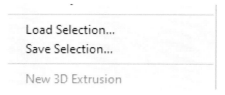

Filter: The Filter menu includes Adobe Photoshop filters. You can access the **Filter Gallery** from this page to obtain a preview of the built-in artistic, brushstroke, distort, sketch, and texture filters.

Convert for Smart Filters allows you to convert an image or element into a smart object before applying your filter effects.

You can also access the **Neutral Filters, 3D, Adaptive Wide Angle, Camera Raw Filter, lens correction, Liquify**, and **Vanishing Point**.

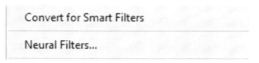

Additionally, there are filters for blur, noise, pixelate, render, and sharpen in this menu. Go to **Filter** > **Other** > **Custom** and click the Load button to find an existing ACF file, or the Save button to create a new ACF file, to save or load a customized Photoshop filter.

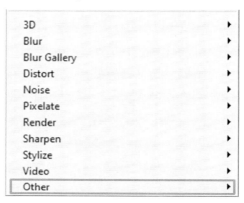

You can also offset horizontally and vertically to give the appearance of an image that has been doubled over by using the Filter menu.

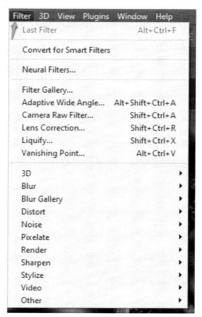

3D: Photoshop is no longer just for flat images. You can generate and edit 3D models for modeling and printing in the recent versions of Photoshop.

The tools required to edit 3D files and optimize their appearance are located in the 3D menu. If you don't have one to work with, you can build 3D objects off of existing layers.

To use the 3D feature in Photoshop, The VRAM of your PC must meet the minimum requirement of the software. Check out Chapter 2 for full details.

View: Tools for controlling how you see things in Photoshop are available on the View menu. You can switch to full-screen mode, enable a ruler, and create guides that you can use for exact positioning.

Zooming options can be found in the View menu in Photoshop. These options include zooming in and out, automatically resizing the canvas to match the size of the screen, displaying the print size, and showing the actual pixel size.

Selection edges, Pattern Review, Print Size, Actual Size, Screen Mode, target paths, notes, layer edges, edit pins, guides, slices, mesh, pixel grid, and brush preview are additional items you can **show** or conceal from the View menu.

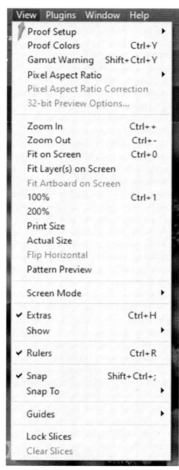

Plugins: The plugins menu in the menu bar gives you direct access to the plugins you have installed or desire to install in your Photoshop Software. Once you click on the Plugins menu, it leads you automatically to the **Plugins Panel**. You can download and install plugins on your device and access them anytime from the Plugin panel.

A plugin is a software add-on that is installed on a program, enhancing its capabilities.

You can download and install plug-ins on your device, and access them anytime from this panel.

Window: The Window menu in Photoshop allows you to customize your workspace by concealing and exposing windows. Use the Window menu to selectively reveal or hide accessible windows as needed because not all of them are always visible.

Toggle any window's visibility or hiding using the Window menu. Examples include Action, Adjustments, Tools, History, Layers, Notes, Paths, Adjustments, Brush, Channels, Color, History, and Channels. It's a good idea to hide them so that your perspective doesn't become cluttered because you won't constantly require them during your projects.

```
        3D
        Actions                          Alt+F9
    ✓   Adjustments
        Brush Settings                   F5
        Brushes
        Channels
        Character
        Character Styles
        Clone Source
        Color                            F6
        Comments
        Content Credentials (Beta)
        Glyphs
        Gradients
        Histogram
        History
```

To change the location of the windows, use the **Arrange** and **Workspace** submenus. However, these menus contain certain pre-set settings for arranging windows in places that are designed to be simpler for various jobs, like painting and typography. You may also drag and drop windows anywhere you choose, including outside of Photoshop's main window.

Help: The menu bar of Photoshop ends with the Help menu. You can access the Photoshop Support Center, Hands-on Tutorials, the new features of Photoshop, about Photoshop, view the version of Photoshop you're using, see which plug-ins are currently loaded, register Photoshop with Adobe, and more.

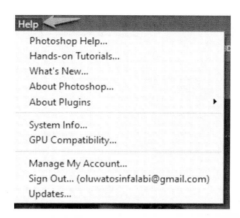

Amazingly, you can modify and add shortcuts to the contents of your menu bar. To edit the contents of your menu bar, follow the instructions below.

To add a panel to your workspace, follow the procedure below,

✦ Select **Windows** from the **Menu bar.**

✦ Select **Workspace** and click on **Keyboard Shortcuts and Menu**.

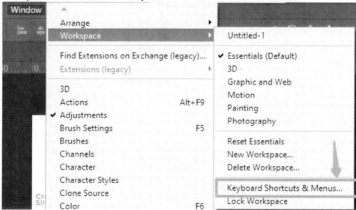

✦ At the upper side of the menu preview, select **Keyboard Shortcuts** to add shortcuts, and **Menus** to edit the contents of your menu.

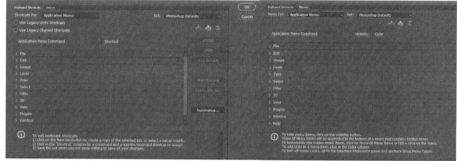

✦ Carefully study the Preview Menu to make edits to your satisfaction.

Photoshop`s Tool Bar

The toolbar for Photoshop is on the screen's left side:

The toolbar typically appears as a single, lengthy column. But by clicking the double arrows at the top, it can be shrunk to a single, shorter column. To switch back to a toolbar with one column, click the double arrows once more:

Let's examine the layout of Photoshop's toolbar. Although the tools may be displayed in a random order, they are organized logically, with related items being grouped.

There are many more tools accessible than what we can see, and each item in the toolbar is symbolized by an icon.

If a tool icon has a little arrow in the bottom right corner, more tools are concealed beneath it in the same location:

Click and hold the tool icon to see the extra tools. Or you can control-click (Mac) or right-click (Windows) the icon. The other tools are listed in a fly-out menu that will appear.

The **default tool** is the one that appears by default in each location in the toolbar. Photoshop, however, won't always show the default tool. It will instead show the last tool you choose.

The Move and **Selection tools** for Photoshop are located at the top. Additionally, the **Crop** and **Slice tools** are directly beneath them. The **Measurement tools** are listed next, then Photoshop's numerous **Retouching and Painting capabilities**.

The tools for **drawing** and **typing** come next. The **Navigation tools** are located at the bottom.

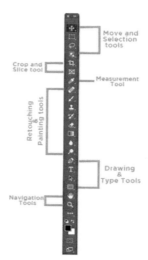

An Overview of Photoshop Tools

Note that, the bracketed letter at the front of each tool is the shortcut for the tools.

Move and Selection Tools

❖ **Move Tool (V):** The Move Tool is used to move layers, selections, and guides inside a Photoshop document. Enable "Auto-Select" to have the layer or group you click on automatically selected.

❖ **Artboard Tool (V):** With the Artboard Tool, you can easily build a variety of web or UX (user experience) layouts for different devices or screen sizes.

❖ **Rectangular Marquee Tool (M):** The Rectangular Marquee Tool produces rectangular selection outlines. While dragging, hold down Shift to make a square selection.

✦ **Elliptical Marquee Tool (M):** Elliptical selection outlines are created using the Elliptical Marquee Tool. To make a selection that is a perfect circle, hold down the Shift key.

✦ **Single Row Marquee Tool**: A single row of pixels in the image is selected from left to right using Photoshop's Single Row Marquee Tool.

✦ **Single Column Marquee Tool**: To choose a single column of pixels from top to bottom, use the Single Column Marquee Tool.

✦ **Lasso Tool (L):** You can create a freeform selection outline around an object using the Lasso Tool.

✦ **Polygonal lasso Tool (L):** To create a polygonal, straight-edged selection outline around an object, use the Polygonal Lasso Tool to click all around it.

✦ **Magnetic Lasso Tool (L):** When using the Magnetic Lasso Tool, the selection outline is fixed to the object's edges while your mouse cursor moves.

✦ **Object Selection Tool (L):** By just dragging a rough selection outline around an object, you can select it with the Object Selection Tool.

✦ **Quick Selection Tool (L):** You can quickly select an object using the Quick Selection Tool by simply painting a brush over it. For higher quality options, turn on "Auto-Enhance" in the Options Bar.

✦ **Magic Wand Tool (L):** With just one click, the Magic Wand Tool in Photoshop may select areas of similar color. The selection of colors depends on the "Tolerance" value in the Options Bar.

Crop and Slice Tools

✦ **Crop Tool (C):** When cropping an image in Photoshop, use the Crop Tool to eliminate any undesirable portions. To crop an image without destroying it, uncheck "Delete Cropped Pixels" in the Options Bar.

✦ **Perspective Crop Tool (C):** Use the Perspective Crop Tool to crop an image while also correcting common perspective or distortion issues.

✦ **Slice Tool (C):** The Slice Tool separates a layout or image into more manageable slices that may be exported and adjusted.

- **Slice Select Tool (C):** To select specific slices made with the Slice Tool, use the Slice Select Tool.

- **Frame Tool (K):** With the new Frame Tool in Photoshop CC 2019, you can insert photos into rectangular or elliptical forms, more like clipping the masks of the photo.

Measurement Tools

- **Eyedropper Tool (I):** The Eyedropper Tool in Photoshop takes color samples from an image. To get a better picture of the color of the sampled region, increase "Sample Size" in the Options Bar.

- **3D Material Eyedropper Tool (I):** To sample material from a 3D model in Photoshop, use the 3D Material Eyedropper Tool.

- **Color Sampler Tool (I):** The color values for the chosen (sampled) area of an image are shown using the Color Sampler Tool. A maximum of four locations may be tested concurrently. View the color information in the Info panel of Photoshop.

- **Ruler Tool (I):** The Ruler Tool calculates angles, distances, and positions. Perfect for placing graphics and other items precisely where you want them.

✦ **Note Tool (I):** Using the Note Tool, you can add text-based notes to your Photoshop document for your use or the use of other people involved in the same project. The PSD file's notes are also retained.

✦ **Count Tool:** Use Photoshop's Count Tool to manually count the objects in an image or to have it count multiple selected areas for you.

Retouching and Painting Tools

✦ **Spot Healing Brush Tool (J):** Blemishes and other minor issues in an image can be swiftly fixed with the Spot Healing Brush in Photoshop. For optimal results, choose a brush size that is just a little bit larger than the spot.

✦ **Healing Brush Tool (J):** Using the Healing Brush, you can paint over larger trouble spots in an image to fix them. Click while holding down Alt (Windows) or Option (Mac), then paint over the problematic area to sample a good texture.

✦ **Patch Tool:** Create a freeform selection outline around a troublesome area using the Patch Tool. Drag the selection's outline over a region with good texture to fix it later.

✦ **Content-Aware Move Tool (J):** To select and move a specific section of an image, use the Content-Aware Move Tool. Photoshop uses components from the surrounding areas to automatically fill in the hole left by the original object.

✦ **Red Eye Tool (J):** The Red Eye Tool eliminates typical red eye issues in a photo brought on by camera flash.

✦ **Brush Tool (B):** The main painting tool in Photoshop is the Brush Tool. Apply it to a layer or layer mask to add brush strokes.

✦ **Pencil Tool:** Another painting tool in Photoshop is the Pencil Tool. However, whereas the Pencil Tool always paints with harsh edges, the Brush Tool can paint with soft-edged brush strokes.

✦ **Color Replacement Tool (B):** To quickly change an object's color to another, use Photoshop's Color Replacement Tool.

- **Mixer Brush Tool (B):** In contrast to the standard Brush Tool, Photoshop's Mixer Brush can mimic aspects of real painting, including color blending and combination as well as paint wetness.

- **Clone Stamp Tool (S):** The most fundamental retouching tool in Photoshop is the Clone Stamp Tool. To cover pixels in another area of the image, it samples pixels from one area of the image.

- **Pattern Stamp Tool (S):** To add a pattern to the image, use the Pattern Stamp Tool.

- **History Brush Tool (Y):** The History Brush Tool adds a snapshot from a previous stage (history state) to the image while it is currently being created. From the History panel, select the previous state.

- **Art History Brush Tool (Y):** Additionally, the Art History Brush adds a stylized snapshot of an earlier historical period to the image.

- **Eraser Tool (E):** Pixels on a layer are permanently erased by Photoshop's Eraser Tool. It can also be used to paint scenes from the past.

- **Background Eraser Tool (E):** By painting over them, the Background Eraser Tool removes similar-colored sections from an image.

- **Magic Eraser Tool (E):** In that, it picks regions of similar hue with a single click, the Magic Eraser Tool is comparable to the Magic Wand Tool. The Magic Eraser Tool, however, afterward permanently erases those regions.

- **Gradient Tool(G):** The Gradient Tool in Photoshop creates gradual color blending between various hues. You can design and create your gradients using the Gradient Editor.

- **Paint Bucket Tool (G):** The Paint Bucket Tool applies your Foreground color or a pattern to a region of similar color. The range of colors that will be impacted in the vicinity of the clicked area depends on the "Tolerance" value.

- **3D Material Drop Tool (G):** The 3D Material Drop Tool is used in 3D modeling and enables you to sample material from one part of your model, mesh, or 3D layer, then drop it into a different location.

- **Blur Tool:** When you use the tool to paint over an area, it blurs and softens it.

✦ **Sharpen Tool:** When you paint over an area, the Sharpen Tool sharpens it.

✦ **Smudge Tool:** The areas you paint over are smeared and smudged by Photoshop's Smudge Tool. It can also be applied to produce the appearance of finger painting.

✦ **Dodge Tool (O):** Use the Dodge Tool to paint over dark areas of the image to make them lighter.

✦ **Burn Tool (O):** The areas you paint over with the Burn Tool will become darker.

✦ **Sponge Tool (O):** Use the Sponge Tool to apply paint over specific areas to alter the color saturation.

Drawing and Type Tools

✦ **Pen Tools (P):** You may create incredibly accurate pathways, vector forms, or selections using Photoshop's Pen Tool.

✦ **Freeform Pen Tool (P):** Draw freehand paths or shapes using the Freeform Pen Tool. As you draw the path, anchor points are automatically added.

✦ **Curvature Pen Tool (P):** The Pen Tool has been streamlined and made easier with the Curvature Pen Tool. Since Photoshop CC 2018.

✦ **Add Anchor Point Tool:** To add more anchor points along a path, use the Add Anchor Point Tool.

✦ **Delete Anchor Point Tool:** Using the Delete Anchor Point Tool, click on an existing anchor point along a path to eliminate it.

✦ **Convert Point Tool:** Using the Convert Point Tool, click on a path's smooth anchor point to change it into a corner point. To change a corner point into a smooth point, click on it.

✦ **Horizontal Type Tool (T):** Use the Horizontal Type Tool, also known as the Type Tool in Photoshop, to add conventional type to your document.

✦ **Vertical Type Tool:** The Vertical Type Tool adds type vertically from top to bottom.

✦ **Vertical Type Mask Tool (T):** The Vertical Type Mask Tool makes an editable selection outline in the form of vertical type, as opposed to adding editable text to your project.

✦ **Horizontal Type Mask Tool (T):** The Horizontal Type Mask Tool produces a selection outline that resembles type, just like the Vertical Mask Type Tool does. The type is added horizontally as opposed to vertically, though.

✦ **Path Selection Tool (A):** To select and move an entire path at once in Photoshop, use the Path Selection Tool (the black arrow).

✦ **Direct Selection Tool (A):** An individual path segment, anchor point, or direction handle can be selected and moved using the Direct Selection Tool (the white arrow).

♦ **Rectangle Tool (U):** With sharp or rounded corners, the Rectangle Tool creates rectangular vector shapes, paths, or pixel shapes. To force the shape into a perfect square, drag while holding down Shift.

♦ **Eclipse Tool (U):** Drawing elliptical vector, path, or pixel forms is possible with the Ellipse Tool. To draw a complete circle, hold down Shift while dragging.

♦ **Triangle Tool (U):** Triangle shapes are created by the Triangle Tool. To draw an equilateral triangle, hold down Shift. To round the corners, select the Radius option.

♦ **Polygon Tool (U):** The polygon tool can draw any number of sides as polygonal shapes. To transform polygons into stars, select the Star Ratio option.

♦ **Line Tool (U):** The Line Tool can draw arrows or straight lines. To alter the line's appearance, change the stroke's weight and color.

♦ **Custom Shape Tool (U):** You can choose and create custom shapes using Photoshop's Custom Shape Tool. Choose from hundreds of pre-built custom shapes in Photoshop or make your own.

Navigation Tools

✦ **Hand Tool (H):** When an image is zoomed in, we can move it around the screen by clicking and dragging it.

✦ **Rotate View Tool (R):** To view and edit the image from various perspectives, rotate the canvas using Photoshop's Rotate View Tool.

✦ **Zoom Tool (Z):** To focus on a particular area of the image, use the Zoom Tool to click on the image. Click with the Zoom Tool while holding down Alt (Windows) or Option (Mac) to zoom out.

To add shortcuts to your tools, do the following.

✦ Select **Windows** from the **Menu bar.**

✦ Select **Workspace** and click on **Keyboard Shortcuts and Menu**.

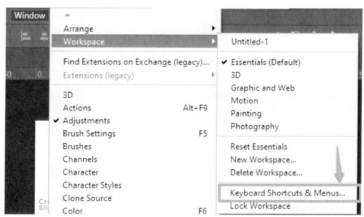

✦ At the upper side of the menu preview, select **Keyboard Shortcuts** to add shortcuts, click on **Shortcut For** and select **Tools.**

✦ Click on the current shortcut commands and change it to the command of your choice.

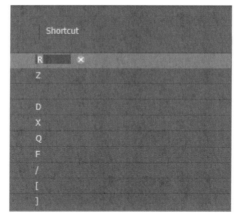

Managing Windows and Panels

Do the following to hide/display all tabs.

- Press the **Tab** key on your keyboard to see or conceal all panels, including the Tools and Control panels.
- Press **Shift + Tab** to see or hide all panels besides the Tools and Control panels.

The tools in the Tools panel can be shown in a single or two columns simultaneously. To do this, follow the instructions given below.

- Click the double arrow at the top of the Tool Panel

Your files/projects are presented in tabs when you open more than one file in Photoshop.

You can arrange your tabs in different ways by following the instructions below.

- Select **Windows** on the **Menu Bar**

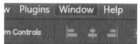

- After selecting **Arrange**, click on any tab options of your choice that suit the project you're working on. You can also try out all the options to find the one that best suits you.

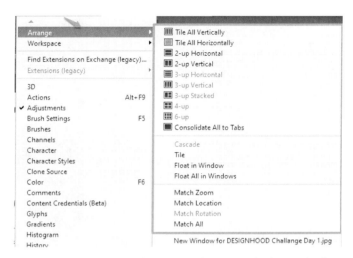

To organize your panels, you can bring them together into docks. A dock is a group of panels. You can create a dock by moving panels to the edge of the workspace until a drop zone appears. If you remove all panels from a dock, the dock disappears.

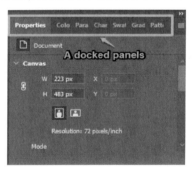

A docked panels

Do the following to dock or undock panels.

- ✛ Drag the panel by its title bar into a dock (a group of panels).
- ✛ Drag the panel by its title bar to undock.
- ✛ To remove a panel and put it into another dock, drag the panel from the original and insert it into the new dock.

Dragging a panel out of its dock and not putting it into another makes the panel float freely. The floating panel allows you to position it anywhere in the workspace. You can stack floating panels or panel groups so that they move as a unit when you drag the topmost title bar.

To collapse and expand a panel, do the following.

✦ Click on the double arrow at the top of the dock.

CHAPTER THREE

BASIC CONCEPTS & PRACTICAL TUTORIALS IN PHOTOSHOP

What you will learn in this chapter.

- **How to create a new document.**
- **The methods of opening file in Adobe Photoshop**
- **How to import images from Lightroom.**
- **The different means of inserting files into a project.**
- **How to work with smart objects.**
- **How to export files out of Photoshop.**

Working with Documents/Projects

Since you are now familiar with Photoshop already, you should be aware that creating a new document in the program is just as crucial as creating the actual artwork. We'll examine *"How to Create a New Document in Photoshop"* in this section.

Creating A New Document

A New Document can be made in Photoshop by selecting one of the available choices. To create a new document, adhere to these steps:

✦ **Launch Photoshop**: Your Home Screen will be open if you are using Photoshop CC. This display is continuously changing.

✦ Press Ctrl + N (Cmd + N) or select **File** > **New**.

✦ The New Document dialog box appears in either case.

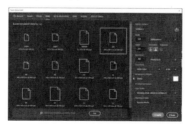

➤ Before starting a new document, make changes to the preset on the right panel. There are various choices available to you:

o "Photo," "Print," "Art & Illustration," "Web," "Mobile," and "Film & Video" are the **preset options**.

o **Name**: Enter a file name for the new document.

o **Width & Height**: Indicate the New Document's size. Select the unit from the pop-up menu as well.

o **Orientation**: Landscape or portrait is the preferred page orientation for the New Document.

o **Artboards**: Choosing this option while creating a new document adds an artboard. It could be added later as well.

o Selecting **Color Mode & Bit** for the New Document. You will primarily employ CMKY (for print purposes), RGB (for digital purposes), and Grayscale (for Black and White) (rarely) in 8-bit out of the five available color modes.

o **Resolution**: The quality of an image is determined by its resolution. You should use 72 PPI for digital purposes (pixel-per-inch). Ideally, you should choose 300 PPI for printing (industrial standard resolution).

o **Background Content**: You can select a different color from the options even though White is the default setting for a New Document.

➤ Click Advanced Choices to specify the additional options.

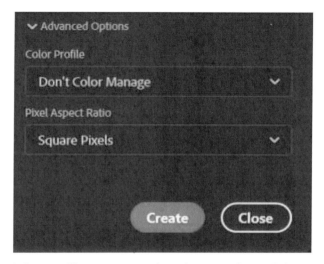

o **Color Profile**: From a wide selection of possibilities, select the color profile for your New Document.

o **Pixel Aspect Ratio**: The proportion of a pixel's width to height.

✥ After configuring all the options, click the "**Create**" button to start a new document.

In Photoshop, there are several ways to insert a picture. Your photographs will always be imported in the greatest quality, whether you just **drag and drop** the image into Photoshop, use **commands,** or **import it from an image database like Lightroom or Desktop File Manager**. However, there are other ways to check the image data already during the import because this does not guarantee incredibly sharp pictures. You will learn about the import options in Photoshop and how to incorporate them into your workflow in this section

The **Open** and **Open Recent** commands can be used to open files. Additionally, you may import files into Photoshop from other Adobe programs including Bridge, Fresco, Lightroom, and Illustrator.

To fully open certain files in Photoshop, such as camera raw and PDF, you must first provide settings and parameters in a dialog box.

Users of Photoshop may open and edit 3D files, videos, and image sequence files in addition to static photographs.

Plug-in modules are used by Photoshop to import and open a variety of file formats. You might need to install the format's plug-in module if a file format is missing from the Open dialog box or the **File** > **Import** submenu.

Do the following to open a file using the **Open Command**.

✦ Choose **File** > **Open**.

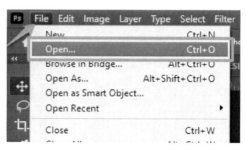

✦ Choose the file name you want to open. Choose the option to display all files from the Files of Type (Windows) or Enable (Mac OS) pop-up menu if the file is missing.

✦ Click **Open**. In some circumstances, a dialog window that lets you configure options specific to the format appears.

Using The Open Recent Command

✦ Select a file from the submenu by selecting **File** > **Open Recent**.

61

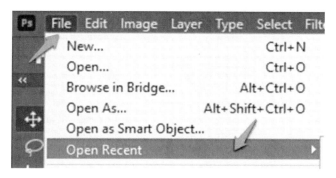

Inserting Images Via Drag & Drop

The simplest technique to load photographs into Photoshop is frequently by utilizing the drag & drop method.

- Open Photoshop and drag a photo from Explorer or your desktop onto the Photoshop user interface.
- Release the left mouse button to create a new document

The resolution, width, length, and color mode of the image are all precisely the same in the document that contains it as they were in the original.

Importing Images from Lightroom

Using Lightroom to examine and organize your photographs and importing them from there is another method for adding photos to Photoshop. By using Adobe Cloud Storage, you may *organize* your images without having to store them on your computer.

- Click the **(+)** symbol in the upper left corner of Photoshop after opening your Photoshop.
- Next, select the picture you want to import into Explorer and press "**Review For Import.**"
- Click **Add Photos** in the top right corner to upload the image to Adobe Cloud. The upper right corner will then display a tiny cloud icon with a spinning blue progress wheel. Your photo has now been posted to the cloud and is prepared to be imported into Photoshop after this icon has vanished after a brief period.

To *import* images from Lightroom, do the following,

- Launch Photoshop and select the Start workspace's **Lr Photos tab**, there is a list of the pictures that have already been added.
- To access the most recent version of your image database, including the most recent photo you uploaded, click the **Refresh** button.

- Now select **Import Selected** after clicking this picture. The image is then downloaded to your local computer where it can be edited as usual.

Inserting Images/Files in existing documents

Similar to the first example, you can drag and drop an image into an existing document to import it. The freshly imported image may be too small to be scaled to the size of the document if it is not displayed over the entire width and height of the document after import (see image). This is so that the photo can be placed into an existing document in its highest quality. The Smart Objects feature in Photoshop is useful in this situation. Photoshop converts a photo into a smart object once it has been imported into a document that already exists. The tiny file symbol in the right-hand corner of the layer's thumbnail serves as a reminder of this. To open the freshly imported photo as a distinct but linked document, double-click the thumbnail.

Inserting Files via Place Embedded

When working on individual photographs without requiring them to interact, having them open in separate documents is fine. Therefore, **Open** command is excellent in certain situations.

What if, however, we wanted to merge or combine the two pictures? Then, it is ineffective to have them in distinct documents. We need a solution to open both photos into a single document instead. In light of this, image placement is necessary. The **Place Embedded** command is used to embed a picture in Photoshop.

↕ In the **File Menu** drop-down, Select **Place Embedded**

✦ Then go to the folder on your PC where your photographs are stored. Select the portrait image by clicking on it, then click **Place**.

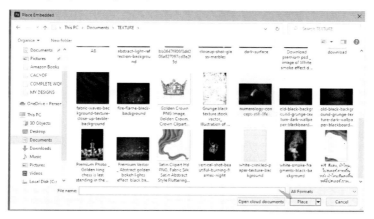

Inserting files via Place-linked

Embedded sets the smart object inside the file, while linked inserts a link to an external file that can be modified. In Photoshop, you can create Linked Smart Objects. The contents of Linked Smart Objects are updated when the source image file changes. For teams or situations where resources need to be used repeatedly across designs, linked smart objects are especially helpful.

Follow these steps to Place Linked:

✦ In the **File** menu drop-down, select **placed linked**

⬦ Select an appropriate file and click **Place**.

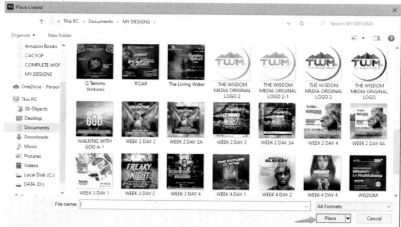

The Linked Smart Object is created and is displayed in the **Layers** panel with a link icon (🔗).

When a Photoshop document that references an external source file is open and that file changes, the relevant Linked Smart Object is automatically updated. However, you can update the Smart Objects when you open a Photoshop document that has Linked Smart Objects that are out of sync:

⬦ Right-click a Linked Smart Object layer and choose **Update Modified Content**.
⬦ Choose **Layer** > **Smart Objects** > **Update Modified Content**

The Layers panel visibly indicates Linked Smart Objects whose Source Images have changed:

⬦ Out-of-sync Linked Smart Objects are highlighted in the Layers panel.

⬦ Linked Smart Objects with missing external source files are highlighted in the Layers panel.

The actions below should be followed to resolve a Linked Smart Object with a missing external source:

- **Resolve Broken Link** can be selected by right-clicking on the Linked Smart Object layer icon.
- Navigate to the missing object's new location.
- Toggle **Place**.

The source files of the Linked Smart Objects can be packaged in a Photoshop document and saved to a folder on your computer. The source files are preserved in the folder along with a copy of the Photoshop document.

- Choose **File > Package**.
- Select a location where you want to place the source files and a copy of the Photoshop document.

Any audio or video Linked Smart Objects in the document are packaged as well.

Place Embedded vs Place Linked

An embedded smart object has no link with the source image once it is placed in Photoshop, unlike a linked smart object. A linked smart object is connected to the source image, and it follows that if the source image is removed, the linked smart object will also be removed. In other words, it breaks.

- When a media file **is placed embedded** in Photoshop, it adds the original size of the smart object embedded to the size of the image it is been added to which results in a large file. While a linked smart object adds only a considerable amount of size to the image it is added to because it is linked to an external image source.
- A linked smart object becomes broken or faulty if its source image is deleted but this does not occur to an embedded smart object because its entirety is in the present file already.
- An embedded smart object is updated automatically if its original image is edited somewhere else and saved but a linked smart object needs to be updated via **Update modified content.**
- An embedded smart object can be linked by clicking on **relink to file.**
- Using **Place Embedded** is best when you're working alone while **Place Linked** is better when you are working with a large team.
- A PSD containing a linked smart object is best transported through the **package** option.

An embedded Smart Object can be changed into a linked Smart Object. The embedded Smart Object's filters transform, and other effects are kept when it is transformed.

Do the following:

- In the Photoshop document, choose a **Smart Object** layer that is embedded.
- Select **Layer > Smart Object > Convert To Linked** from the menu.
- Choose the computer's location where you wish to save the source file. Give the file a name and an extension that is supported. For illustration, link file.jpg

Do the following to filter your layer panel with smart objects.

- Choose **Smart Object** from the filtering pop-up menu in the Layers panel.

- Click one of the following icons:
    - Filter for up-to-date Linked Smart Objects

    - Filter for out-of-synch Linked Smart Objects

    - Filter for missing Linked Smart Objects

    - Filter for embedded Smart Objects

An embedded or connected smart object can be broken down into its layers and then immediately imported into a Photoshop project. If the Smart Object has more than one layer, the additional layers are unpacked into a new layer group in the Layers panel. When you unpack, Transforms and Smart Filters on Smart Objects with more than one layer are lost.

- From the Layers panel, pick the **Smart Object layer**.
- Attempt one of the following:

o Click the Smart Object layer with the right mouse button (Windows) or control button (Mac) and choose **Convert To Layers** from the context menu.
o Select **Layer** > **Smart Objects** > **Convert To Layers** from the menu bar.
o Click **Convert To Layers** in the **Properties panel**.
o Select **Convert To Layers** from the **Options menu** of the Layers panel.
o In the Layers panel, the layers are unpacked into a layer group.

If you no longer need to edit the Smart Object data, you can rasterize the contents of a Smart Object to a standard layer. After a Smart Object has been rasterized, the transforms, warps, and filters that have been applied to it are no longer editable.

↕ Select the Smart Object, and choose **Layer** > **Smart Objects** > **Rasterize**.

Do the following to convert the contents of a smart object.

↕ Choose **Layer** > **Smart Objects** > **Export Contents** after selecting the Smart Object from the Layers menu.
↕ Click **Save** after deciding where to save the Smart Object's data.

The Smart Object is exported by Photoshop in its placed format (JPEG, AI, TIF, PDF, or other formats). The Smart Object is exported in PSB format if it was built from layers.

Working with Smart objects

Layers with picture data from raster or vector images, such as those in Photoshop or Illustrator files, are called "Smart Objects." Smart Objects keep the original qualities of an image's source content intact, allowing you to change the layer without causing any damage.

The contents of an image can be **embedded** into a Photoshop document. You can make **Linked** Smart Objects in Photoshop that have content that is referenced from outside picture files. When a source image file changes, a Linked Smart Object's contents are updated.

Linked Smart Objects in a Photoshop document are different from duplicated instances of a Smart Object. A known and welcome notion for web designers linked smart objects allow you to use a shared source file across several Photoshop documents.

Benefits of Smart Objects

Smart Objects allow you to:

- Make non-destructive changes. The actual image data is unaffected by the transformations, so you can scale, rotate, skew, distort, perspective transform, or warp a layer without losing quality or information.
- Work with vector data that Photoshop would often rasterize, such as Illustrator's vector art.
- Nondestructive filtering should be done. Smart Object filters can be changed at any moment.
- Edit one Smart Object and all of its associated instances will be automatically updated.
- Link or unlink a layer mask to the Smart Object layer before applying it.
- Try out different layouts using low-resolution placeholder images that you will later replace with the finished products.

The truth to know about smart objects is that Painting, dodging, burning, and cloning operations cannot be applied directly to a Smart Object layer; instead, they must be transformed into a standard layer first, which will then be rasterized. You can edit the contents of a Smart Object, clone a new layer above the Smart Object layer, update copies of the Smart Object, or build a new layer to carry out actions that change the pixel data.

Placed Embedded and **Placed Linked** are the two major ways to insert a smart object into a document in Photoshop.

Exporting Files out of Photoshop

There are three main ways to save your work while dealing with photos in Photoshop: **Save**, **Save As,** and **Export**. All of these options will preserve a copy of your image, but they differ significantly in several important ways.

The main method for storing your work in Photoshop is **Save**. This action allows you to save your project as a PSD file and allows you to save changes too.

To use **Save**, do the following.

- Select **File** from the **Menu Bar** and click on **Save**.

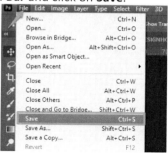

By selecting **Save As**, you make a new copy of your image with a different file name. If you wish to make several copies of an image or save your work in different file formats, this is helpful.

To use **Save As**, follow the procedure below

✦ When you are ready to export your file, simply Select **Save A**s from the **File** menu drop-down.

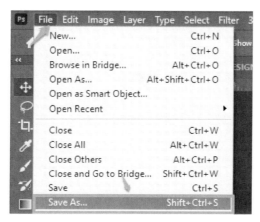

✦ Select your storage, either **save on your computer** or **save to Creative Cloud**.

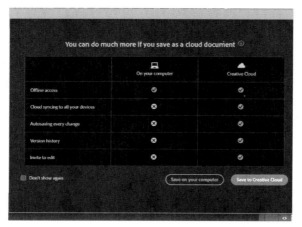

✦ Either of the options you choose, the next preview box allows you to select the file format you desire to save your document in, then select **save**

The backup method for saving your work in Photoshop is called export. When you use Export, a new version of your image is produced with the same.

The following are the formats you can save your files in.

- **Photoshop Document (PSD):** The PSD format is likely the most significant of all the file formats that Photoshop supports. PSD, which stands for "Photoshop Document," is the default file type for Photoshop. Layers, layer masks, adjustment layers, channels, paths, and other potent features that Photoshop provides us with are all fully supported by PSD, one of the few file types that can. It works as your working file as well. Regardless of the file format, an image was initially saved in, when we view it in Photoshop, Photoshop temporarily turns it into a PSD file so we may edit it using all of Photoshop's tools, commands, and features. The only true drawback of PSD files is that especially when working on an image with hundreds or even thousands of layers, the file size can grow significantly. The most crucial file you can have is your PSD file, therefore make sure you save a master duplicate of your work as a PSD file so you can always access it in Photoshop when you need to!

- **Joint Picture Experts Group (JPG or JPEG):** For images with a lot of colors, such as photographs and continuous tone images, this format is ideal. JPEG can preserve crystal-clear image quality while achieving great compression ratios.

- **Graphical Interchange Format (GIF):** Even older than JPEG, the GIF file format, which stands for Graphics Interchange Format, is the preferred one for web graphics. Not web photos—notice that I said web graphics. The maximum number of colors that GIF files can display is 256, a much smaller number than the hundreds of colors required to accurately recreate a photographic image (and far less still than the millions of colors supported by the JPEG format). On the other hand, the GIF format is crucial for web design. The files work particularly well for web page layouts, banners, and buttons when they have a lot of solid colors. GIF files are supported by all popular web browsers, and because of their modest file sizes, they load rapidly. Simple animations can also be made by site designers using GIFs. GIF

- **Portable Network Graphics (PNG):** PNG (Portable Network Graphics) was created to dispense with the GIF format (PNG also stands for "PNG not GIF"). The PNG format outperforms the GIF format in almost every manner, even though it never happened and GIF files are still widely used today. Even the JPEG format is enhanced by it. PNG files support up to 48-bit color, which gives us more than 1 billion potential colors, but JPEG files only support 24-bit color (16.7 million colors). This format exploits patterns in the image to compress the image and is a lossless storage format. PNG less compression is perfectly reversible, which means the uncompressed version of the picture in the image is similar to the original. PNG is a fantastic option for preserving digital photographs as originals of excellent

71

quality. The drawback is that PNG does not support CMYK color, which prevents commercial printers from using them, and it is not as extensively supported as the JPEG format. Even though the image quality isn't as outstanding, the JPEG format is still more practical and easy for everyday viewing and sharing of your digital photos.

- **TIFF (Tagged Image File Format):** TIFF (Tagged Image File Format) is another excellent option for image archiving since it offers lossless compression, allowing you to preserve pictures with the best possible image quality. TIFF files, like PSD files, are one of the few file types that support all of Photoshop's features. TIFF files can be relatively huge, especially when compared to JPEG files, therefore the quality comes at a cost. The most widely used format for photographs intended for commercial printing, TIFF is compatible with almost all page layout applications, including QuarkXPress and InDesign. This format can be based on either a lossy or lossless compression method, making it very flexible. The image itself contains information about the compression method. TIFF files typically use a lossless picture storing format and are therefore extremely large.

- **Encapsulated PostScript (EPS):** Another long-established print industry-standard format is EPS (Encapsulated PostScript), but usage has been dwindling over time. In the conventional sense, EPS files are not image files. They instead include a set of guidelines for how a printer should print the image. The "encapsulated" element means the files are virtually locked and can no longer be updated until they are reopened in Photoshop, however, they can still be imported into most page layout programs. Unless your commercial printer specifically requests it, you probably won't use it very often.

- **Portable Document Format (PDF):** The Portable Document Format (PDF) is gaining popularity as an excellent option for saving photographs intended for printing, even though the majority of people are already accustomed to using PDF files for viewing, sharing, and printing electronic documents (thus the name). The PDF format supports and maintains all of Photoshop's functionality, including the usage of spot colors, which the EPS format does not. This is similar to how the PSD and TIFF formats do. You can choose between lossless ZIP compression and JPEG compression in PDF. JPEG has a Quality setting that allows you to balance image quality and file size. The image can be viewed by anyone who has the free Adobe Reader software installed on their computer using the PDF format.

To use **Export**, follow the procedure below,

- Select **Export** from the **File** menu drop-down

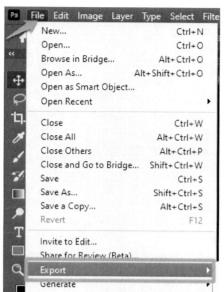

✦ Select how you want to export your work in the next drop-down menu

✦ You can explore the options and pick the one that suits your desire.

CHAPTER FOUR

DIGITAL IMAGES AND COLOR MODES IN PHOTOSHOP

What you will learn in this chapter.

- **What digital images are.**
- **What image resolutions are.**
- **The Color modes that are available in Photoshop and how to effectively apply them**

Having Sufficient Knowledge of Digital Images

A digital image is made up of picture components, commonly referred to as pixels.

The shorthand for "picture element" is "pixel," because pixels are the insignificant constituent parts of all digital images. A digital image is created from individual pixels, much as how a painting is created from individual brush strokes.

In Photoshop, the pixels are typically too small to see when examining a picture at a regular zoom setting (100 percent or less). Instead, we observe what appears to be a continuous image, where light, shadows, colors, and textures all combine to produce a scene that closely resembles what would be seen in the actual world.

Based on their method of storage, digital images can be classified into two categories: **vector images** and **raster/bitmap images**. Understanding the features of each format will help you decide which is ideal for your project because each one has advantages and disadvantages that are relevant to particular situations.

- **Vector Image:** Vector images are stored in the form of mathematical lines and curves. Information like length, color, thickness, etc., is stored in the form of a vector. These images can be displayed in any size, any resolution, and on any output. Unfortunately, Photoshop uses pixels to produce images and is raster-based. Photoshop is made specifically for altering and producing raster-based art or photographs. The program was first created for photographers, but over time it has expanded to support many types of artists in producing a wide range of work. Raster images will be well discussed in the next type of digital images and their nature in Photoshop but here, in this section, let us explore Vector Images.

  When a design needs to be scalable, vector files are the best option because they maintain sharp detail at any size. A great option for digital images like logos is the vector format. The benefits of the vector format will be permanently lost if a vector file is converted to a raster file.

  SVG, EPS, and EMF are common vector file extensions. = Vectors

- **Raster/Bitmap Images**: Raster files also referred to as bitmaps, perform best when it comes to storing and displaying high-quality photographs. Whether they be digital or print, the majority of images are in the raster file format.

  You can alter individual pixels within a raster file to alter the appearance of a photograph using software like Adobe Photoshop.

  A rectangular array of sampled data, or pixels, is what makes up a bitmap or raster image. The number of pixels in these pictures is fixed. Mathematical interpolation is used when a raster image is zoomed, the quality of a zoomed-in image declines after a certain zooming factor value. The sensing device determines the resolution of a bitmap image.

  Common bitmap or raster image formats include BMP, GIF, PNG, TIFF, and JPEG.

Practical Applications

You can see pixels in Photoshop by using the Pixel Grid. Follow the instructions below to enable and disable the pixel grid.

- Select the **View Menu** in the **Menu Bar**,
- Select **Show**, and then choose Pixel Grid- To turn it back on, just select it again

Another practical application of pixels in Photoshop is image resolution.

Image Resolution is the number of pixels in the image measured from top to bottom (Vertical) and left to right (Horizontal). Based on current picture size, image resolution determines how large or tiny photos will print and how they will appear on the screen. Digital image resolution can also refer to the quantity of visible detail described in pixel dimensions, such as 640 by 480 pixels, the horizontal dimension preceding the vertical. Image resolution is typically described in PPI, which refers to "pixels per inch"

Higher resolutions mean that there are more pixels per inch (PPI), resulting in more pixel information and creating a high-quality, crisp image.

Images with lower resolutions have fewer pixels, and if those few pixels are too large (usually when an image is stretched), they can become very blurred and unclear.

The number of pixels that will be crammed onto each inch of paper, both vertically and horizontally, determines how big a picture will print. Because of this, the resolution value is expressed as "PPI," or pixels per inch. Since there are only so many pixels in the image, the image will print smaller the more we squish those pixels together on the page.

Understanding Color Modes

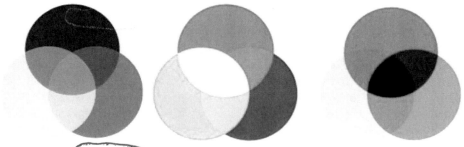

The number of color channels in a color mode affects how a color's constituent parts are blended.

For designers to optimize each stage of the design process, differentiating the color modes is essential. Selecting the right color mode for your design can also help in conveying your message and tone. The common color modes will be identified in this lesson, and we'll go over when to use them in your designs.

Photoshop Elements supports **CMYK**, **RGB**, **Bitmap**, **Grayscale**, **Indexed**, **Duotone**, **Lab**, and **Multichannel** color modes. The color mode to use for a design is determined by the context of use by your user. Each of the Color modes is aimed at a peculiar purpose.

RGB Color Mode

Photoshop RGB Color mode uses Red, Green, and Blue colors to provide a wide range of color variants. The RGB Color mode is only supported on digital formats, such as those found on computer monitors, mobile devices, and television screens. Although RGB is a standard color model, the exact range of colors represented can vary, depending on the application or display device. The RGB Color mode in Photoshop varies according to the working space setting that you specify in the Color Settings dialog box. The RGB profile uses an additive approach to make color by combining light instead of utilizing ink to create hues. White is created when all RGB colors are present at their maximum intensity, while black is created when all colors are absent. Because of this, when you power off your device, the screen displays black due to a lack of RGB color. These RGB foundation colors are what cause the color displays on your screen.

RGB should only be utilized for digital designs. When designing for websites, applications, digital design, social media, or online marketing, set your documents to RGB. RGB should be used for any image you design on a computer screen.

Although you can design in CMYK for a digital design, the limited gamut range of CMYK will limit your color possibilities.

CMYK Color Mode

The four colors that make up the CMYK color mode—Cyan, Magenta, Yellow, and Key (Black)—combine to create a variety of tones. The majority of printer types can use this four-color technique. Essentially, printed images are a collection of four-color dots that are placed on top of one another to produce various shades and gradations. Printing uses the CMYK color profiles and produces dots per inch. CMYK is a common color model, although depending on the press and printing circumstances, the precise range of colors represented can change.

The Process color uses four ink colors — cyan, magenta, yellow, and black — printed as millions of tiny, overlapping dots that blend to create the full-color spectrum.

Only use CMYK for designs that will be printed. When designing business cards, letterheads, posters, brochures, and packaging, set your papers in CMYK. When preparing an image for process color printing, use the CMYK mode instead of RGB since converting an image to CMYK causes a color separation. If you begin with an RGB image, it is recommended to edit in RGB first and convert to CMYK once you have finished editing. Before exporting a document for printing, kindly check the color mode once more for the benefit of both you and the printer. This will avoid the potential for imbalanced color when converting RGB colors into CMYK counterparts.

LAB Color Mode

The human sense of color serves as the foundation for the LAB color mode, often known as CIELab (pronounced See-Lab). The color mode has two channels for color (A and B) and one channel for lightness (L). The Green-Red Axis channel (A) and Blue-Yellow Axis channel (B) have a range of +127 to -128 while the Lightness channel (L) has a range of 0 to 100. The Lab mode depends on three color attributes, such as saturation, hue, and lightness.

LAB color would be an excellent option for designing branded products like t-shirts, coffee mugs, or banners because it will guarantee that the colors look precisely the same.

To predictably convert a color from one color mode to another, color management systems use LAB as a color reference. Additionally, you can use LAB to enhance the vibrancy and naturalness of the colors in your photographs.

Indexed Color Mode

8-bit picture files with up to 256 colors are created using the Index color mode. Only digital formats, such as those found on computer monitors, mobile devices, and television screens, support this color mode. According to Adobe, a color table is created when an image is converted to index color, storing and indexing the image's colors. The software selects the nearest color or employs a dithering effect to approximate the color if one from the original image does not appear in the database.

Index color can reduce file size while maintaining the visual quality required for digital presentations, websites, and mobile applications, despite having a constrained color palette. Index color mode is therefore the best for optimizing images. You should temporarily switch to RGB mode for substantial editing because this mode only allows for a limited amount of manipulation.

It is a good option for digital presentation and designing mobile applications and websites.

Grayscale Color Mode

The Grayscale mode is composed of various shades of gray. Up to 256 different shades of gray can be present in 8-bit graphics. A grayscale image's pixels each have a brightness value between 0 (black) and 255. (white). The number of shades in an image is significantly more in 16- and 32-bit images than it is in 8-bit photos.

Grayscale should only be used for digital and print designs. Use greyscale in digital forms to convey a particular tone in your designs. To cut costs and use as little ink as possible when printing, utilize grayscale.

Another feature of the Grayscale color mode in Photoshop is that the bitmap, multichannel, and duotone color modes cannot be accessible to an image unless the image is converted to the grayscale color mode.

Bitmap Color Mode

Bitmap mode uses one of two color values (black or white) to represent the pixels in an image. Images in Bitmap mode are called bitmapped 1-bit images because they have a bit depth of 1. Pixels in the Bitmap mode, also known as line art, are black and white. Bitmap images don't have hues or shades of gray. This technique applies to both print and digital media. Black and white values serve as a representation of an image's pixels in digital formats. In print media, the overall image is represented by white paper and black ink dots

A Bitmap Image

The bitmap should only be used for digital and print designs. You can use a bitmap to simulate a line drawing or a hand-drawn sketch in both forms. It can also be used to simulate the appearance of an old illustration. When viewed on a screen, bitmap graphics may appear to have jagged edges; yet, with a high enough print resolution, they often print quite cleanly and smoothly.

Before you can use the bitmap color mode on an image in Photoshop, you need to switch your color mode either from RGB or CMYK (depending on the color mode you`re designing with) to the grayscale color mode.

Duotone Color Mode

The duotone mode uses one to four bespoke inks to produce monochrome, duotone (two-color), tritone (three-color), and quadtone (four-color) grayscale images. Duotone color mode is only accessible for use on an image if it is first converted to a grayscale color mode.

Duotone effects are a great way to incorporate and reinforce your brand and its colors throughout your work and your website.

Multichannel Color Mode

Multichannel Color mode is useful for specialty printing since each channel has 256 levels of gray. The following formats are available for saving multichannel mode images:

Photoshop, Large Document Format (PSB), Photoshop 2.0, Photoshop Raw, or Photoshop DCS 2.0.

When converting photos to Multichannel mode, keep in mind these rules:

- Layers get flattened because they lack support.
- Spot color channels are created in the converted image from the original image's color channels
- Cyan, magenta, yellow, and black spot channels are produced when a CMYK image is converted to Multichannel mode.
- Cyan, magenta, and yellow spot channels are produced when an RGB image is converted to Multichannel mode.
- An RGB, CMYK, or Lab image that has a channel deleted automatically switches to Multichannel mode, flattening the layers.

Save a multichannel image in Photoshop DCS 2.0 format before exporting.

CHAPTER FIVE

LAYERS; ONE OF THE FINEST TOOLS IN PHOTOSHOP

What you will learn in this chapter.

- **How layers work in Photoshop.**
- **The types of layers and how to use them.**
- **How to use adjustment layers.**
- **How to use adjustment presets.**
- **How to use Auto Contrast, Auto Tone and Auto Color.**
- **How to work with blending modes in Photoshop.**
- **How to spice up your projects using Photoshop**

Understanding Layers

Ever wonder how Photoshop manages to achieve such amazing results? Although there are other ways to change images, professionals use layers in Photoshop on almost every project. Learning how to use layers is perhaps the most important thing you can do to improve your Photoshop skills. This webinar will discuss the purpose of layers, the many types of layers, as well as the principles of layer creation and usage.

Layers in Photoshop are individual slices of information that can be stacked or rearranged to create the composition of your image. Layers in Photoshop allow you to work non-destructively by stacking images on top of other images without interacting and mixing the pixels of images. Multiple photos can be stacked, text can be added to an image, vector graphics can be added, etc. using layers.

There are several types of layers in Photoshop and they can be divided into three major groups: **Content layers, Empty layers** & **Adjustment layers.**

♦ **Content Layers**: different forms of content, including images, text, and shapes, are contained within these levels.

   o **Background Layers**: The layer that contains a picture by default when you first open it in Photoshop is known as the Background Layer. Because the Background Layer is protected, many filters and effects cannot be used on it. Background layers are always referred to as "Background" and are by default locked or protected. You can edit the layer name and other details in the dialog box that appears when you double-click the layer name in the Layers Palette to unprotect the background. After clicking OK, your layer will be unprotected.

- o **Image layer**: Any picture-related information is contained in image layers. A new layer is always created as an Image Layer by default. A preview of the contents of the layer can be found in the Layer Thumbnail of Image Layers.

- o **Type Layer**: Only live type is present in Type Layers. The Type Tool can be utilized to create and change them.

- o **Fill Layer**: Solid colors, gradients, and patterns can all be used as fill layers. By selecting **Layer** > **New Fill Layer** and selecting either Solid Color, Gradient, or Pattern, you may create a new fill layer.

- o **Shape layer**: Shapes created using the Shape Tools are stored in Shape Layers. Select the layer and Shape Tool to get editing options for a shape layer.

- ✦ **Empty Layers**: these are layers that have no elements in them. They are considered empty.

✦ **Adjustment Layers**: These layers allow you to apply adjustments to the layers beneath them, such as brightness or saturation, to the layers. Adjustment layers are a kind of non-destructive editing because they don't alter the source image.

Layer Basics

The Layers panel lets you view, make, and modify layers. Although you can always go to **Window > Layers** to check it's on, this is typically located in the lower-right area of the screen.

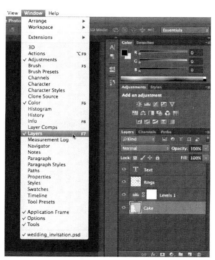

The Layer Panel is by default accessible in the primary workspace. However, if you misplace it, you can reactivate it by pressing the f7 key on your keyboard. We will manage and modify the layers using the layers panel.

The layers panels are shown in the image below.

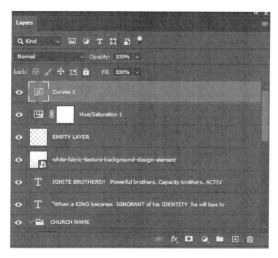

The Photoshop Layers feature has several parts. Let's examine all the elements and various Layer types:

- **Thumbnail**: A thumbnail is a small image that contains the layer's content. It is visible on the layer.

- **Visibility Toggle**: In the layer panel, you can see each layer has an eye symbol. You can enable or disable the layer by clicking on the eye icon.

- **Layer Name**: This displays the layer's name. The type of layer it is will by default define the name.

  By double-clicking the layer name, entering a new name, and pressing the ENTER key, you can rename a layer.

- **Opacity and Fill**: The opacity (or transparency) of a layer can be altered using the commands Opacity and Fill. Both commands function identically, with one exception. Opacity will change the transparency of everything that is in the selected layer. Fill will change the transparency of whatever is filling the layer but will ignore any effects that have been applied to it.

✦ **Blending Modes**: Layers' look and display are impacted by blend modes. Blending modes are divided into five groups, each of which has a particular impact on the layer. The easiest approach to using blending modes is to combine them and try out various combinations.

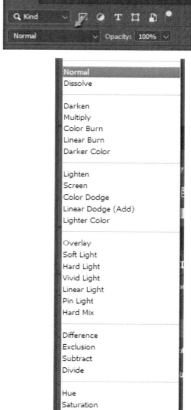

◆ **Locking Layers**: When using Photoshop, the ability to lock layers can be useful. The layer or layer contents can be locked in several different ways. By choosing the layer, followed by the type of lock, each layer can be locked. Here are the various lock kinds.

◆ **Layer Buttons:** Many of these buttons carry out operations that are also available in the Layers Palette for convenience and ease of use but in other places inside the application. Below is a list of these buttons.

1. **Link Layers**: Layers can be linked together by selecting two or more layers and clicking this button. They will all move together if they link.

2. **Add a new layer style**: You can add a new layer style using this button without first going to Layer and choosing Layer Style from the menu.

3. **Add Layer Mask**: The selected layer will receive a new layer mask when you click Add layer mask.

4. **Create a new fill or adjustment layer**: By pressing this button, you can add a new layer style without using the Adjustments Palette.

5. **Create a new group**: Creating a new group is as simple as clicking this (aka folder). To arrange the layers, drag them into this group.

6. **Create a new layer**: A new, empty layer will be created when you click this.

7. **Delete layer**: Select one or more layers and click on this button to delete.

If you ever need to combine multiple layers or flatten the entire image, use the merge and flatten commands

Merge Layers
Merge Visible
Flatten Image

Follow the instructions below.

✦ After choosing the layers, right-click your mouse and select **Merge Selected** from the drop-down menu. All of the selected layers will be blended into one

✦ Combine or merge only visible layers () by selecting "**Merge Visible**" from the context menu.

✦ Right-click any layer's layer name, then choose "**Flatten Image**" to flatten the entire image.

Blending Options...
Edit Adjustment...

Duplicate Layers...
Delete Layers

Convert to Smart Object

Rasterize Layers
Rasterize Layer Style

Disable Layer Mask
Enable Vector Mask
Create Clipping Mask

Link Layers
Select Linked Layers

Copy Layer Style
Paste Layer Style
Clear Layer Style

Copy Shape Attributes
Paste Shape Attributes

Merge Layers
Merge Visible
Flatten Image

Working with layers

As you are aware, the appearance of your image is affected by the order in which layers are stacked. You must understand how to shift layers so that you can adjust their arrangement as necessary.

The Layer mask is an essential part of a layer for non-destructive editing. It is used to paint on the mask to show and reveal the image components. A reversible method to conceal a portion of a layer is to apply masks to the layer. Compared to permanently removing or deleting a portion of a layer, this approach offers more editing freedom.

To add a layer mask to a layer, do the following,

- Select the layer you desire to mask
- Click on the layer mask icon () at the bottom of the layer panel.

You can conceal any portion of a layer by painting black on the layer mask with a brush, and paint color white on the layer mask to reveal any portion of a layer that is previously hidden.

Each color that can be used to paint layer masks—black, white, or grey—has a specific purpose.

- BLACK to conceal: Adding black to a layer mask makes the mask-containing layer invisible while revealing the contents of the layer below.
- WHITE to reveal: When white is added to a layer mask, the layer with the mask is simply displayed.
- GREY is used to indicate the degree of opacity: Adding various shades of grey causes the layer with the mask's opacity to change.

Photoshop is a sophisticated photo editor; typically, when we select a new tool and begin sketching on it, a new layer is created. For instance, adding text to an image using the text tool will result in the creation of a new layer.

To manually add a new layer, press the **Ctrl** + **Shift** + **N keys** or click the new layer icon() located at the bottom of the layer panel. It will ask for a new layer, which you should name and then click **OK** to create. We can specify this layer's opacity, color, and color modes.

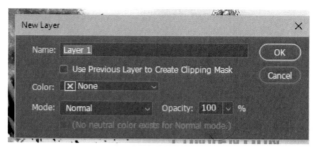

The method of deleting a layer is as simple as creating a new layer. Do the following to delete a layer.

- ✦ Right-click the layer in the **Layers Panel**.
- ✦ Choose **Delete** from the drop-down menu or click on the **Delete icon** located at the bottom of the Layers panel(🗑).

In Photoshop, you must have at least one layer selected to carry out the majority of operations. Do the following to select the layer(s).

- ✦ Simply click on a layer in the Layers Panel to select it. When a layer is selected, it will turn blue as shown on the right.
- ✦ Holding down the CMD (Mac) or CTRL (Windows) key while clicking on each layer you want to have selected will select several layers.
- ✦ Select the first layer, hold down the SHIFT key, and select the last layer to select many layers in succession.

As you are aware, the arrangement of your layers will determine how your image will look. You must be able to move layers to be able to change their arrangement as needed.

✤ Choose the layer or layers you want to move.

✤ Drag the layer to the desired location by clicking and holding down the mouse button. Between layers, a thick line will show to show where the layer will be dropped. Release your mouse button when the layer is in the desired location and it will go there.

There are typically multiple layers in a Photoshop project, which can rapidly get confusing and make it difficult to find anything. Fortunately, there are certain tools available to aid in the discovery of various levels.

✤ You can choose to search layers by **Kind, Name, Effect, Mode, Attribute**, or **Color** by clicking the Search Dropdown ( ).

✤ Use the options to the right of the **Search** Dropdown after choosing a search strategy to choose additional attributes to include in the search results.

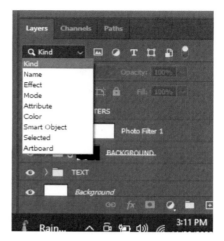

The ability to create folders also referred to as groups, is another tool that can help you and your layers stay organized. Layers can be added to a group and arranged however you like.

- ✤ By selecting the "**Create a new group**" button (📁) at the base of the layers palette, a new folder can be created.
- ✤ To include layers in the group, drag them onto the group folder layer.
- ✤ To rename the Group Name, double-click on it in the Layers Palette.

Right-click the layer group and choose **Ungroup Layers** to remove all of the layers from it. All of the layers will be ungrouped from the group, and the group will be deleted.

Do the following to change the size of your layers` thumbnails.

- ✤ Choose the Panel option (rectangular lines in the top-right corner) from the layer panel.

- ✤ then select the thumbnail size to modify the layer's thumbnail size.

91

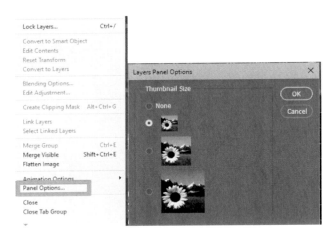

To change the contents of thumbnails, do the following.

✦ To change the thumbnail content, select the **Panel Options** from the Layers panel and select the entire document.

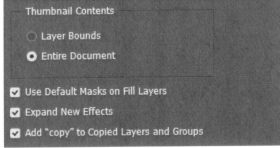

✦ Now, select the layer bounds to specify the thumbnail content on the layer.

To make several tweaks without impacting the original layer, we can duplicate a layer by following any one of these options.

✦ Right-click the layer and choose "**Duplicate Layer**" to make a copy of it.

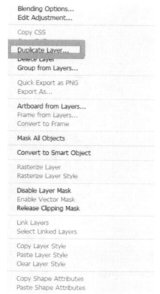

Blending Options...
Edit Adjustment...

Copy CSS

Duplicate Layer...
Delete Layer
Group from Layers...

Quick Export as PNG
Export As...

Artboard from Layers...
Frame from Layers...
Convert to Frame

Mask All Objects

Convert to Smart Object

Rasterize Layer
Rasterize Layer Style

Disable Layer Mask
Enable Vector Mask
Release Clipping Mask

Link Layers
Select Linked Layers

Copy Layer Style
Paste Layer Style
Clear Layer Style

Copy Shape Attributes
Paste Shape Attributes

- Select the layer you desire to duplicate, drag it, or use the arrow key as you hold the **Alt key (Window)/ Option key (macOS)**

- Select and drag the layer you desire to duplicate to the **create new layer icon (** ▣ **)**

- Select the layer you want to copy and then use Ctrl J(Windows)/ Cmd J(macOS)

- Select your layer and use the copy-and-paste shortcut. Ctrl C to copy and Ctrl V to paste on Windows, Cmd C to copy, and Cmd V to paste on macOS.

Two or more levels or groups can be linked. Layers are linked together to form a relationship, which they will maintain until we unlink them. To linked layers, we can apply or move transformation.

- Select the layers or groups you want to link, then click the link icon at the bottom of the layer panel.

- Select the layers or groups you want to unlink, then click the link button once again. It will remove the layer links.

- The connected layers can be temporarily disabled. Temporarily shift-click the link icon to unlink them, then repeat the process to relink them.

To hide/show a layer, do the following.

- Click the eye icon next to the selected layers to make a layer invisible. Click on this symbol once more to reveal the layer.

Working with Adjustments Layers

Edits/Adjustments can be to images or layers in Photoshop in two ways, **destructively** or **non-destructive**. A destructive edit makes permanent changes to an image thereby altering the original image data. You can reverse the changes except you undo your actions using Ctrl+ Z. Non-destructive edits only make adjustable changes to a project due to the presence of the layer mask.

What are Adjustments Layers?

A series of Photoshop editing tools called **Adjustment Layers** can be used to play with an image's color and tone without permanently altering it. The original image can always be restored by editing and removing adjustment layers. Adjustment layers like the name imply are special kind of layers in Photoshop that allows you to make modifications to an image on another layer but still apply to the image without total alteration. Adjustment layers give you greater control and flexibility over image edits than direct adjustments

(handwritten note:) Adjustment layers = = editing tools not permanent alterings modifications

By default, an adjustment layer affects all layers below it, although you can change this behavior by clicking on the clipping icon() below the properties panel. When you create an adjustment layer, the Layers panel displays a white box representing the adjustment for that layer.

To use the Adjustment layers, follow either of the following procedures:

From the Layers panel

✦ Move down to the **Layer Panel** and **select** a circular logo with its semi-area-shaded black

✦ Select the adjustment you want to use.

From the Menu Bar

✦ Select **Layers** from the **Menu Panel**

✦ From the **Layer**'s display, Click on **New Adjustment Layers**

95

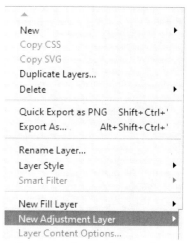

✦ You can then choose the adjustment layer of your choice.

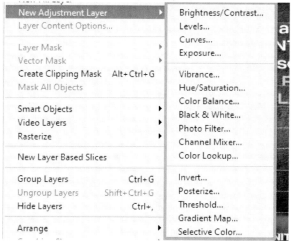

From the Adjustments Panel

✦ Another way to access your Adjustment layers is to pick them from the **Adjustment Panel.** The Adjustment features in the **Adjustment Panel** are adjustment layers automatically.

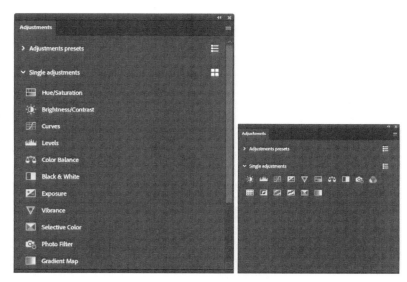

Note that you can only access your Adjustment Panel if you have placed it in your workspace from the **Window** Option.

You may need to familiarize yourself with the terms below to know how some adjustment features operate.

- ✦ **Color grading**: Color grading in Photoshop is all about adjusting and making modifications to the colors and tones (levels of brightness) of an image.
- ✦ **Highlights:** consists of the brightest areas and it permits modifications to these areas
- ✦ **Shadow:** Unlike the Highlights, it consists of the darkest area of an image and allows changes to be made in these areas.
- ✦ **Mid-tones:** are areas that are between the darkest and the brightest areas, more like grey. Like the other features, Mid-tones also permit modifications to their areas.

Adjustment Presets

Adjustment Presets are one the most recent features introduced to Photoshop. They are housed in the same panels as the adjustment layers.

Adjustment Presets are already made effects created by Adobe to spice up user`s experience while working with Photoshop.

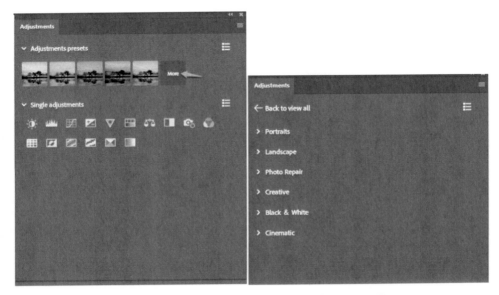

NB: Click on "**more**" to have access to all Adjustment Presets.

The Adjustment Presets in Photoshop are divided into **Portraits**, **Landscape**, **Photo Repair**, **Creative**, **Black and White**, and **Cinematic**.

All adjustment presets are made up of two or more adjustment layers. Learning how to use the adjustment layers will guide you on how to use adjustment presets effectively. Follow me as we dive deeper.

Adjustment Layers

Listed below are the adjustment layers available in Photoshop

Brightness/Contrast: This refers to the overall lightness or darkness of an image. The difference in brightness between two objects or locations is known as a contrast. You can use this adjustment layer to increase/reduce the brightness and contrast of an image or photograph. Follow the instructions below to do that.

- Select **Brightness/Contrast** from the adjustment panel.

✦ Adjust the sliders to make edits to your desire.

The **contrast slider** is used to alter the shadows in your image, while the **brightness slider** is used to adjust the highlights in your image. Every pixel becomes lighter when the brightness is increased, while light parts become lighter, and dark areas become darker when the contrast is increased.

Levels: The tone range and color balance of an image can be modified with the levels tool. It accomplishes this by modifying the brightness levels of your image's shadows, mid-tones, and highlights. Levels Presets can be saved and then easily applied to further images. Follow the instructions below to use the Levels Adjustment.

✦ Select "Levels" right from the adjustment panel,

- ✦ You can make adjustments to your images in the levels panel by twerking the **eyedropper icons** and the **triangular icons** in the panel preview like it is in the image below.

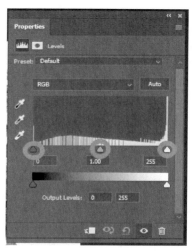

Curves: This adjustment feature works as same as the levels but is far more advanced and used to edit a section of an image rather than the whole of it. It allows you to select the region of the tonal scale you want to change, whereas the Levels adjustment allows you to proportionally adjust all the tones in your image. The highlights are shown on the Levels graph in the upper-right corner, while the shadows are shown in the lower-left corner.

When your image's contrast is off, use one of these modifications (levels or curves) to alter your tone (either too low or high).

If you need to make a general change to your tone, the Levels Adjustment is effective. You should use Curves if you want to make more focused adjustments. This applies if you wish to make changes to only a portion of the tonal range or only the light or dark tones.

To use the curve adjustment, follow the procedures below,

- Select curve adjustment in the adjustment panel

- The tone range of your image is represented by a diagonal line on a graph that appears when you click the curves adjustment (see left). The y-axis displays the updated adjusted values, while the x-axis displays the image's original values. The tonal range of the image is represented by a strip that runs along each axis and has a gradient from black to white.

- Click to add points to the line of your graph to improve the overall quality and contrast of your image. After adding a point, you can use your mouse to move it up or down. Your image will become darker if you pull the point down, and brighter if you bring the point up.

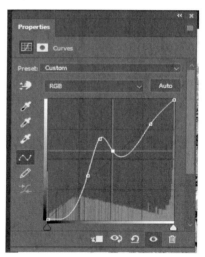

Exposure: This is the amount of light a photo is taken in. The exposure adjustment enables you to determine the amount of exposure in an image.

Select **Exposure** from the adjustment panel

With the use of the Exposure, Offset, and Gamma sliders, you may change the exposure levels. Only the highlights of the image will be altered by exposure, the mid-tones will be altered by offset, and the dark tones will only be altered by gamma.

Vibrance: This is a clever feature that amplifies the intensity of the image's more subdued hues while leaving the already saturated hues alone. Additionally, it keeps skin tones from being unnaturally saturated and saturated. The saturation control, which modifies the strength of all hues, is another feature of the vibrance adjustment. Colors and skin tones can very easily appear strange due to saturation. It is advised to use the **Hue/Saturation** adjustment rather than the **Vibrance** adjustment to modify the saturation of the image.

To use the Vibrance adjustment, follow the procedure below,

- Click on Vibrance in the adjustment panel

- The vibrance of an image is altered in two different ways using this adjustment layer. The **Saturation slider** enhances each color's saturation in the image uniformly. The **Vibrance slider** makes subtle changes to the saturation levels of all the colors, concentrating on the ones that are least saturated and avoiding oversaturating skin tones.

Hue and Saturation: With the help of hue and saturation, you can modify the overall color hue and level of saturation in your image. It allows you to change the hue, saturation, and brightness of your entire image or just a certain color range.

Follow the procedures below, to use the Hue/Saturation adjustment.

- Select Hue/Saturation from the adjustment panel

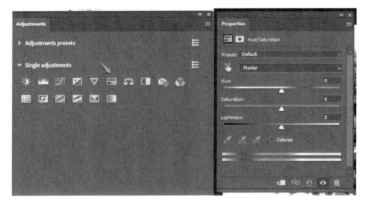

✦ By maintaining "Master" in the dropdown selection, you can alter the hue (color) of your entire image (this is set by default). As an alternative, you can specify the specific color whose hue you want to alter. Reds, Yellows, Greens, Cyan, Blues, or Magentas are your color options.

✦ You can deal with specific colors and modify the overall **lightness** of your image in addition to changing the image's obvious **hue** and color **saturation**. Remember that altering an image's overall saturation has an impact on your tonal range.

✦ The colorize feature in the hue/saturation adjustment allows you to change the colors in an image to a single color.

Color Balance: General color correction is accomplished via the **Color Balance** adjustment. **Using Color Balance is a making attempt to find a balance between two complementary colors. For instance, RGB colors complement CMY colors.** Color Balance uses inversely complementary colors: cyan and red, magenta and green, and yellow and blue. As a result, if an image has too much cyan, the cyan value must be reduced, which will raise the red value. Don't modify the Color Balance too much or you can accidentally change one erroneous color for another.

Follow the procedure below, to use the color balance adjustment:

✦ Select Color Balance from the adjustment panel

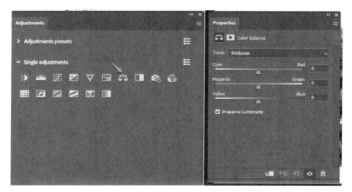

✥ To determine the tonal range you want to modify, first choose either Shadows, Midtones, or Highlights.

✥ To maintain your luminosity values, select the Preserve Luminosity checkbox.

- Slider movement should be made in the direction of the color you want to intensify and away from the color, you want to dim. As the hue of your image changes, keep the tonal balance consistent.

Black and White or tint or grayscale

Black and White: This adjustment layer, as its name suggests, makes it simple to convert your photos to grayscale or completely add a color tint.

The processing of black-and-white images can be done in a variety of ways. One of the best ones is the black-and-white Photoshop Adjustment Layer. To improve your black-and-white conversion, you can lighten or darken certain color ranges. For instance, if you want the greens in your color image to shine out more in the black-and-white version toggle that slider. By making some hues lighter or darker, you can increase or decrease the contrast.

- Select the black and white adjustment from the adjustment panel

✥ You can make particular color ranges lighter or darker to enhance your black-and-white conversion. Toggle that slider, for example, if you want the blues in your color image to stand out more in the black-and-white version. You can alter the contrast by making some hues lighter or darker.

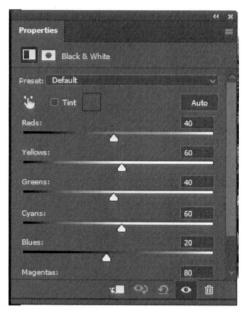

Photo Filter: Different color filters are added to your photo using Photo Filter. The Photoshop Photo Filter Adjustment Layers can be a quick and simple technique to alter the mood of a picture or fix a color cast. They're based on conventional filters from the era of film photography, but Photoshop gives you access to a much wider variety of filter types.

You have the option of rolling your filters or using some of the common ones at the preset density. This is a simple program to use, and I'll quickly go over the numerous options you have at your disposal so you can use them to edit your photographs and provide some instances of how the settings might result in various results.

To use the Photo Filter adjustment, follow the procedure below;

✥ Select Photo Filter from the adjustment panel

✦ It is simple to switch the filter by picking it from the list by clicking the drop-down menu adjacent to the **Filter button**. Simply select the **Filter button** if the drop-down is inactive and grayed out.

✦ If you want to get creative, you can select your color for the filter, Simply select the color box below the drop-down menu to accomplish this, and a new dialog box or picker (Photo Filter Color)" will appear. This displays the well-known ...hop color picker, and as you choose a new color, the Color button turns on ...the drop-down menu turns gray. Real-time impacts of your chosen color on ...your image are visible.

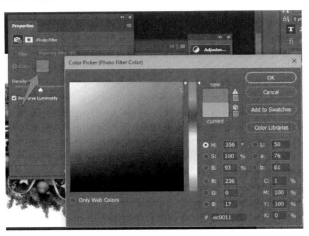

❖ The Density slider makes it simple to adjust the filter strength. 25% is the default setting for this. Increase the amount of the new color added to the image by dragging this slider to the right. Decrease the effect by dragging it to the left for softer results.

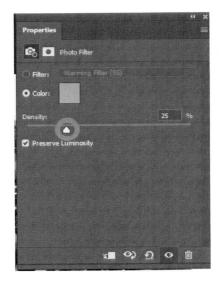

♦ The Preserve Luminosity check box, the last parameter, maintains the overall brightness of your shot when selected.

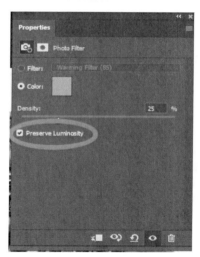

Chanel Mixer: The Red, Green, and Blue channels can be readily mixed to alter the colors of an image using the channel mixer adjustment layer. it also contains a monochrome mode to produce black-and-white images. It is a simple process that allows any element in your image to be changed to any other color in the rainbow. The Channel Mixer adjustment is frequently used to produce high-quality conversions from color to black and white, correct color casts, and accentuate the color.

Follow the procedure below, to use the Channel Mixer adjustment;

♦ Select the Channel Mixer in the adjustment panel

- Click on the drop-down menu adjacent to the **output channel** to select the channel you desire to modify.

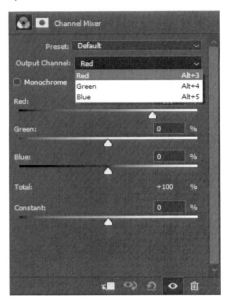

- Toggle the color sliders until you get your desired color or input a value in the rectangular box at the upper right of each slider to get the desired colors.

- The overall value for each channel must be monitored; try to keep it within 100%. When you exceed 100%, a warning is shown since this indicates that the color output is too bright or dark, and you are losing data in the highlights or the darkest sections. A negative value indicates that you are adding more color to the channel, whereas a positive value indicates that you are removing color.

Color Lookup: The power of LUTS, or look-up tables, is unlocked by the color look-up adjustment layer. This is a strong operation that lets you assign preset recipes to replicate different film stocks or create sophisticated color effects, as well as transfer color information between programs.

You can apply a variety of pre-packaged "looks" from this adjustment to your image. These many looks are loaded using three options: **3DLUT File, Abstract**, and **Device Link**.

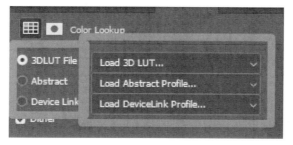

Each "look" uses a lookup table to remap the colors in your image (LUT). You can even make your LUTs in Adobe Speedgrade and import them into Photoshop to stylize your photographs. These effects are rather interesting.

Follow the instructions below to use the color lookup adjustment:

- Select the color lookup adjustment from the adjustment panel

✦ Pick a Color Lookup table from the list in the **Properties panel**. Pick a Color Lookup table from the list in the Properties panel.

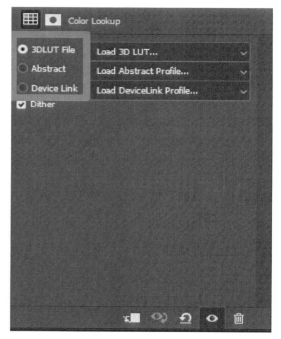

✦ From the Color Lookup table you selected, pick a preset and try out many presets to determine which one best suits your image.

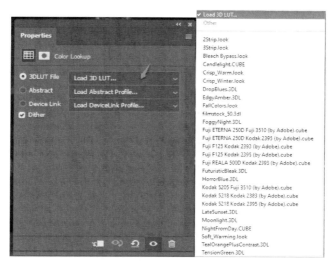

❖ To fine-tune the adjustment, use the Layers panel's Layer **Blend Mode** and **Opacity** options.

Invert: This adjustment layer flips the colors in your image to create a photo-negative appearance.

To use the invert adjustment layer, follow either of the instructions below

❖ Select the invert adjustment layer in the adjustment panel.

❖ Another way to use the invert adjustment is to add a layer mask to your image.

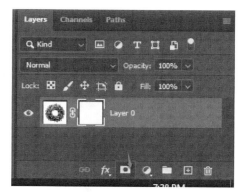

✦ Click on your layer mask.

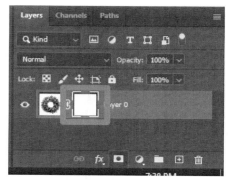

✦ Then use the keyboard shortcut **Command + I (Mac)** or **Control + I (Windows)**

Posterize: This feature allows you to evaluate the pixel colors in a specific area of a picture and lower the number of colors while preserving the original image's appearance. Applying this modification gives images a painted-wood block-color appearance. By limiting the brightness settings that are available in your image, the ***Posterize Adjustment*** Layer provides you with a flat, poster-like finish.

By choosing the number on the levels slider, you can add or remove detail from an image as you see fit. Your image has more detail the higher the number. Your image has less detail the lower the number.

When you wish to screenprint your artwork, this can be useful. Black and white tones can be restricted.

Follow the instructions below to use the posterize adjustment.

◆ Select the posterize adjustment from the adjustment panel

◆ In the properties panel you will notice that the level slider is drastically reduced, toggle the slider or input the desired value till you are satisfied with the effect.

Threshold: This feature converts your photo to a monochrome version (a black-and-white image). Your image turns black and white when you choose Threshold from the list of Photoshop Adjustment Layers. You can choose how many pixels are black or white by adjusting the Threshold Level value.

To use the threshold adjustment, follow the procedure below;

✦ Select the threshold adjustment from the adjustment panel

✦ By toggling the Threshold Level value, you can select the number of pixels that are black or white till your desired result is obtained.

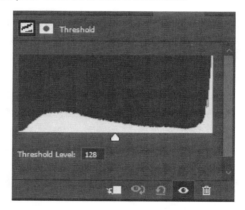

Selective Color: This adjustment layer alters a single primary color's intensity while leaving the other primary colors in your image unchanged. This is an adjustment feature that allows you to change the amount of process color in each of the primary color components in an image selectively. For instance, you can modify the amount of CMYK in the Red color in an image separately without affecting the other colors. Selective color also allows you to remove color in specific areas of your image.

To use the selective color adjustment, follow the instructions below:

✦ Select the selective color adjustment from the adjustment panel

❖ Click on the box adjacent to the color button to choose the primary color you want to modify.

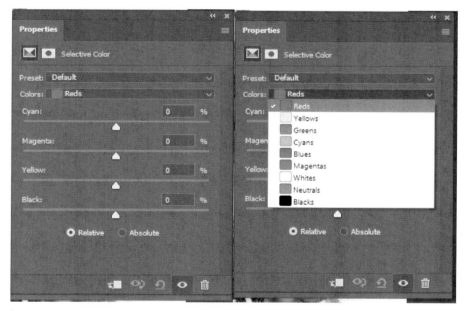

❖ Toggle the color sliders to make adjustments to our image till you get your desired result.

Gradient Map: The gradient map applies the gradient by using the brightness and darkness values in the image as a map for how the gradient colors are applied, in contrast to a gradient fill, which fills an area by using a linear or radiant blend of colors. The effects permit the duotone effect in Adobe Photoshop. You can color grade images as an overlay, and color replace an image with multiple, usually two, tones. Color replacing includes black and white images, but this tool allows you to choose any two colors rather than the base two tonalities. Based on the kind of result you desire, to maximize the duotone effect of this feature, it is advisable to first desaturate your image.

To use the gradient map adjustment, follow the instructions below:

♦ Select the gradient map adjustment from the adjustment panel

- There are several distinct gradients included with the Gradient Map tool, all of which may be customized in the gradient editor box. Click on the gradient fill, to pick the colors you want for it.

- If you desire to invert the colors of your gradient, check the **Reverse box** in the **gradient editor box**.

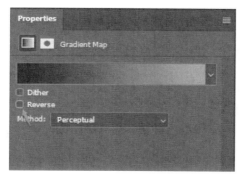

- Then click **OK** after you are satisfied with your result

The Three Auto-Commands

The Auto adjustment commands are three one-tap instructions that can be used to correct three color, tone, and contrast imbalances in your images:

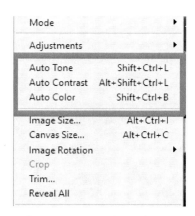

There are three auto image adjustments in Photoshop and they are **Auto Tone**, **Auto Contrast,** and **Auto Color**. These three Auto commands each perform unique manipulations on color channels (these grayscale images), yielding unique outcomes. Auto image adjustments are also known as Auto- Commands because they are entirely automatic, they carry out their complete operations as soon as they are selected Let`s quickly do a study on each auto command.

Behind The Scene- How the Auto Contrast, Auto Tone, And Auto Color Operate

Although understanding the mechanics of the Auto commands isn't strictly necessary to utilize them, it can be helpful to know why one of the three commands performed better than the others. We must have a basic understanding of **Photoshop's color channels** to fully comprehend how the Auto commands operate.

Every other color is created from some combination of these three primary hues, which are the fundamental colors of light. **Red, green**, and **blue** are combined equally and at their maximum intensities to create white. Every hue and shade between black and white is created using some combination of red, green, and blue. Black is the total absence of all three main colors. Red and green, for instance, can be combined to create yellow. Magenta is produced when you combine red and blue, while cyan is produced when you combine green and blue. There are millions or possibly billions of colors when all the red, green, and blue hues are combined.

Using **color channels**, Photoshop combines the three main colors. Three channels are available: one for red, one for green, and one for blue. These color channels can be found in the **Channels panel**, which by default sits next to the Layers panel. To access it, open the **tab** at the top of the panel group:

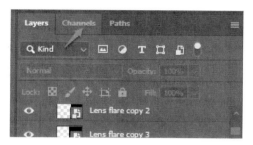

The Red, Green, and Blue channels are visible in this image, coupled with what appears to be a fourth channel, RGB at the top, But don't be misled by the RGB channel. It hardly even qualifies as a channel. Red, Green, and Blue, or RGB, is the simple composite of the Red, Green, and Blue channels, which together provide our full-color image:

It could come as a bit of a shock to you, but the Red, Green, and Blue channels' preview thumbnails don't show any color at all for those three channels! Each one is a grayscale image instead. In reality, if we examine them more closely, we can observe that the grayscale image of each channel differs from the others. Simply click on each channel to see a preview of how it will appear in your document.

Photoshop uses the brightness values in the grayscale image to determine how much color to mix into each area. The grayscale in each color channel is slightly different from the other because it shows how the color in each channel is mixed with it. For instance, In the Red Channel, the brighter the area, the redder is added to the full-color version, while the darker areas have less red mixed into them. In the grayscale image, pure white parts have pure Red added to them, whereas black areas have no Red at all.

In the Green Channel, Green is added to places of greater brightness while being subtracted from those of greater darkness. Purely black areas have no green at all, but any areas of pure white have green injected at full intensity.

124

In the Blue Channel, darker sections receive less blue in the full-color version, while lighter sections show areas where more blue is mixed in. Pure white areas have full-intensity blue applied to them. Pure black areas have no blue at all.

In most cases, the Blue Channel is always the channel with the darkest areas.

Auto Contrast.

The simplest and most uncomplicated of the three is Auto Contrast. By treating all three color channels as if they were a single grayscale image when we choose Auto Contrast, Photoshop simply converts the darkest pixels to pure black, and the lightest pixels to pure white, and redistributes all intermediate tonal values in between. An image with better overall contrast is the outcome of this operation. It's vital to remember that Auto Contrast does not alter the colors of the image because it views all three color channels as a single composite image. It merely increases overall contrast, making it a suitable option for photographs that don't have any color issues and simply need a little more "pop."

To use the Auto Contrast adjustment, follow the procedure below:

⬥ Open the **Image Menu** from the **Menu Bar** and select **Auto contrast.** The command carries out the operation immediately.

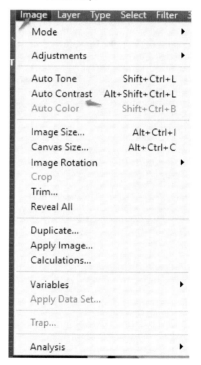

Auto Tone

The only significant difference between Auto Tone and Auto Contrast is that Auto Tone additionally converts the darkest pixels to pure black, and the lightest pixels to pure white, and redistributes all other tonal values in between. The Red, Green, and Blue channels each get their unique bump in contrast since it does so on a channel-by-channel basis. By altering the color channels separately from one another, we can effectively alter how the colors are combined, we know that Photoshop utilizes the brightness values in each color channel to determine how much of each hue to mix into the full color. This means that, in contrast to Auto Contrast, which only enhances overall contrast, Auto Tone modifies the color of the image. Auto Tone might be able to remove any unwanted color cast from your image. Unfortunately, Auto Tone might end up adding a color cast to an image that didn't have one at first.

✦ Open the Image Menu from the Menu Bar and select Auto Tone

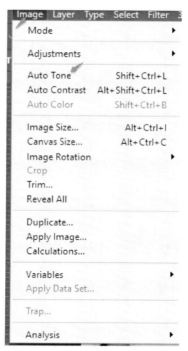

Auto Color

Auto Color and Auto Tone are related. The Red, Green, and Blue channels are once again affected separately and independently of one another since it also changes each channel's darkest and lightest pixels on an individual basis from white to black and from black to darkest to lightest. Auto Color, however, goes one step further. By neutralizing the image's mid-tones, it attempts to fix any undesirable color cast rather than just redistributing all the other tonal values in between. This makes Auto Color the greatest option for simultaneously increasing contrast and fixing color issues most of the time (but not always).

To use the Auto Color adjustment on your work, Open the **Image Menu** from the **Menu Bar** and select **Auto Color**.

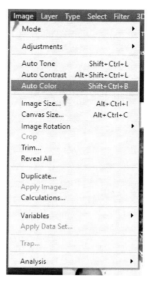

Blending Modes in Photoshop

Layers are combined using mathematical equations called blending modes that take into account the color, saturation, brightness, or a combination of these factors.

Without using layer masks, you can utilize blending modes to apply textures, overlays, or target modifications to particular portions of your image. The use of Blending Modes is highly recommended for producing nondestructive effects. Only the visual output is altered by the blend you apply. The Blending Mode is constantly changeable or reversible.

The blending mode is located at the upper-left of the layer panel, adjacent to the opacity slider.

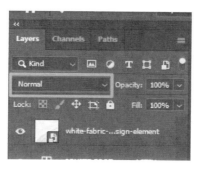

You need at least two layers for Blend Modes to function. The Base layer is the layer underneath, while the Blend layer is the layer above. The blend operation used on the Blend layer is determined by the Blending Mode.

Groups are set to Pass Through by default, and all Layers are set to Normal by default.

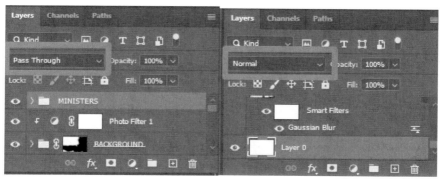

There are 27 blend modes in Photoshop and they are grouped into six categories. Each group of blending modes is categorized based on similar operations that they perform and they are; **Normal Modes, Darken Modes, Lighten Modes, Contrast Modes, Comparative Modes,** and **Composite Modes.**

(Image source from https://www.photoshopessentials.com/photo-editing/layer-blend-modes/intro/)

Understanding Each Blending Mode for their uniqueness

Before we move into each blending mode, let`s quickly discuss an important aspect of blending modes; **Neural Colors**.

❖ **Neural Colors**: Some blending modes provide "Neutral Colors," or colors that blend without having any impact. Neural colors are also known as shades of grey
White, for instance, serves as the Multiply Blending Mode's Neutral Color. With Multiply, any white pixels on a layer will turn translucent.
Black serves as the Screen Blending Mode's Neutral Color. With Screen, any black pixels on a layer will turn translucent.

Normal Blending Modes

The blending methods used by the blending modes in this category do not combine pixels. Instead, the mix between layers is controlled by the Opacity slider.

❖ **Normal:** The default Blending Mode for Photoshop layers is "Normal." Without applying any arithmetic or algorithms, opaque pixels will obscure the pixels below them. To reveal or "blend" the pixels with the layer beneath, you must lower the Opacity.

Keyboard shortcut: Option Shift N (Mac) or Alt Shift N (Windows) (macOS)
Neutral Color: none

✢ **Dissolve**: Additionally, pixels are not blended in the dissolve blending mode. When the layer's Opacity or Fill is decreased, Dissolve just makes the pixels underneath visible. Dissolve never displays a blend of two colors; it always displays the base color. Without anti-aliasing, the effect will appear harsh and grainy.

A pseudo-random noise dither pattern whose intensity depends on the Opacity reveals the pixels underneath.
Keyboard shortcuts: Alt Shift I (Windows) or Option Shift I (macOS)
Neutral Colors: none

Darken Blending Modes

The Blending Modes in the Darken category will, as the name suggests, make the colors of the result darker.

For all of the Blend Modes in this category, white is a Neural Color. Anything darker than white will make white pixels transparent, and anything lighter than white will make the pixels below it darker.

✢ **Darken**: The base color or blend color is chosen by the Darken Blending Mode depending on whatever RGB channel's brightness values are darker.

This blending mode merely compares the base and blend colors, keeping the one that is the darkest of the two. It does not merge pixels. There is no change if the base layer's color and the blend layer's color match.
Keyboard Shortcut: Alt Shift K (Windows) or Option Shift K (macOS)
Neutral Colors: White
* Not available in the Lab Color Space.

✢ **Multiply**: One of the most used Blending Modes in Photoshop is multiply. You have probably used it a lot already. With this Blending Mode, the blend color increases the luminosity of the base color. There is always a darker color as a result. Black pixels remain unchanged when white is present.

Depending on the blend layer's luminosity values, multiply can result in a wide range of darkening levels. A wonderful Blending Mode for shadows or dimming pictures is *Multiply*.
Keyboard Shortcut: Alt Shift M (Windows) or Option Shift M (macOS)
Neutral Colors: White

✢ **Color Burn**: By raising the contrast between the base and blend colors, the Color Burn Blending Mode produces a darker image than Multiply, with more intensely saturated mid-tones and fewer highlights.
Keyboard Shortcut: Alt Shift B (Windows) or Option Shift B (macOS)
Neutral Colors: White

* Not available in the Lab Color Space or 32-Bi32-bit.

❖ **Linear Burn**: Based on the value of the blend color, Linear Burn reduces the brightness of the base color. The outcome is less saturated than Color Burn but darker than Multiply. Compared to the other Blending Modes in the Darken category, Linear Burn also produces the most contrast in darker colors. Keyboard Shortcut: Alt Shift A (Windows) or Option Shift A (macOS)
Neutral Colors: White
* Not available in 32-Bi32-bit.

❖ **Darker Color**: Darker Color Blending Mode and Darken are extremely similar. Pixels are not blended in this blending mode. The darkest of the two is kept and just the base and blend colors are compared.
Darker Color examines the sum of all the RGB channels, whereas **Darken** examines each RGB channel separately before blending them.
Keyboard Shortcut: None
Neutral Colors: White
* Not available in the Grayscale Mode.

Lighten Blending Modes

This category's Blending Modes are complementary to or the antithesis of those in the Darken category. Brighter colors will result from using the Lighten Blending Modes.

For all of the Blend Modes in this category, black is a Neural Color. Any color that is lighter than black will make black pixels transparent, while anything darker than black will make the pixels below it brighter.

❖ **Lighten**: The lightest of the two bases and blend colors are retained when using the Lighten Blending Mode. If the two colors match, then nothing changes. Lighten blends the pixels by taking into account each of the three RGB channels separately, similar to the Darken blend mode.
Keyboard Shortcut: Alt Shift G (Windows) or Option Shift G (macOS)
Neutral Colors: None
* Not available in the Lab Color Space.

❖ **Screen**: Another of Photoshop's most used Blending Modes is Screen. Always a brighter hue is the end outcome. While the brighter pixels remain the same, black becomes transparent.
The screen is an excellent Blending Mode for brightening photos or adding highlights because it may provide a wide range of brightness levels depending on the luminosity values of the blend layer.
Keyboard Shortcut: Alt Shift S (Windows) or Option Shift S (macOS)
Neutral Colors: Black

* Not available in 32-Bi32-bit.

- **Color Dodge**: By reducing the contrast between the base and blend colors, the Color Dodge Blending Mode produces a brighter appearance than Screen, producing saturated mid-tones and blown-out highlights.
  Keyboard Shortcut: Alt Shift D (Windows) or Option Shift D (macOS)
  Neutral Colors: Black
  * Not available in the Lab Color Space or 32-Bi32-bit.
- **Linear Dodge (Add)**: Compared to Screen or Color Dodge, Linear Dodge (Add) yields effects that are comparable but stronger. This blending mode examines the color data in each channel and boosts the brightness of the base color to reflect the blend color. Nothing changes when black is blended in.
  Keyboard Shortcut: Alt Shift W (Windows) or Option Shift W (macOS)
  Neutral Colors: Black
- **Lighter Color**: Lighter Color and Lighten are pretty similar. Pixels are not blended in this blending mode. Only the base and blend colors are compared, and only the brighter of the two is kept.

  To create a final blend, Lighten looks at each RGB channel, whereas Lighter Color examines the composite of all the RGB channels.
  Keyboard Shortcut: Alt Shift (Windows) or Option Shift (macOS)
  Neutral Colors: Black
  * Not available in the Grayscale Mode.

Contrast Blending Modes

This category's Blending Modes are a hybrid of the Darken and the Lighten categories.

Photoshop determines whether the colors are lighter or darker than 50% gray. Photoshop uses a Darkening Blending Mode when the color is darker than 50% gray. Photoshop uses a Brightening Blending Mode when the color is brighter than 50% gray.

50% gray is a Neural Color for all Blend Modes in this category, except Hard Mix.

- **Overlay**: Another of the most widely used Blending Modes in Photoshop is Overlay. On colors that are brighter than 50% gray, Screen is used at half power. Additionally, on colors that are darker than 50% gray, multiply at half strength. 50% gray turns translucent in and of itself. You should be aware that "half-strength" does not refer to opacity at 50%. Consider altering mid-tones as another way to think about overlay. Light tones shift the mid-tones to brighter colors, while dark tones shift them to darker colors

  Overlay and the other Contrast Blending Modes differ from one another in that it bases their calculations on the brightness of the colors in the base layer. The

brightness of the blend layer serves as the foundation for all other contrast blending modes' calculations.
Keyboard Shortcut: Alt Shift O (Windows) or Option Shift O (macOS)
Neutral Colors: 50% Gray
* Not available in 32-Bit Mode.

✦ **Soft Light**: Overlay and Soft Light are extremely similar. Depending on the luminance levels, it either applies a darkening or a brightening effect, albeit much more subtly.
Consider Soft Light to be a gentler variation of Overlay without the jarring contrast.
Keyboard Shortcut: Alt Shift F (Windows) or Option Shift F (macOS)
Neutral Colors: 50% Gray
* Not available in 32-Bit Mode.

✦ **Hard Light**: Making its computations, Hard Light mixes the Multiply and Screen utilizing the brightness values of the Blend layer. The base layer is used in the overlay. Hard Light typically produces powerful results, and you'll frequently need to lower the Opacity to achieve better ones.
Although Hard Light could seem to share certain similarities with Soft Light, this is untrue. They are a component of the first group of computed blending modes and are considerably more closely related to overlay.
Keyboard Shortcut: Alt Shift H (Windows) or Option Shift H (macOS)
Neutral Colors: 50% Gray
* Not available in 32-bit Mode.

✦ **Vivid Light**: Vivid Light can be compared to an extreme form of Overlay and Soft Light. Anything that is 50% gray or lighter is brightened, while anything that is 50% gray or darker is darkened. Vivid Light produces a strong result, therefore you'll probably need to lower Fill or Opacity.
The fifth of the eight special blending modes, called Vivid Light, blends differently depending on whether Fill or Opacity is changed.
Keyboard Shortcut: Alt Shift V (Windows) or Option Shift V (macOS)
Neutral Colors: 50% Gray

✦ **Linear Light**: Linear Light employs a combination of Linear Dodge (Add) and Linear Burn on lighter and darker pixels, respectively. Since Linear Light produces a powerful result, you will probably need to lower Fill or Opacity. Linear Light employs a combination of Linear Dodge (Add) and Linear Burn on lighter and darker pixels, respectively. Since Linear Light produces a powerful result, you will probably need to lower Fill or Opacity.
Keyboard Shortcut: Alt Shift J (Windows) or Option Shift J (macOS)
Neutral Colors: 50% Gray
* Not available in the Lab Color Space or 32-Bit Mode.

- **Pin Light**: Pin Light is an aggressive Blending Mode that simultaneously blends Darken and Lightens. It eliminates any mid-tones
  Keyboard Shortcut: Alt Shift Z (Windows) or Option Shift Z (macOS)
  Neutral Colors: 50% Gray
  * Not available in 32-bit Mode. mid-tones and can produce patches or blotches.
- **Hard Mix**: Hard Mix applies the blend by adding the value of each RGB channel of the blend layer to the corresponding RGB channels in the base layer. The resulting image loses a lot of detail, and the color choices are limited to black, white, or one of the six primary colors (yellow, cyan, magenta, or cyan).
  Keyboard Shortcut: Alt Shift L (Windows) or Option Shift L (macOS)
  Neutral Colors: None
  * Not available in 32-Bit Mode.

Inversion Blending Modes

To generate the blend, the inversion blending modes search for differences between the base and blend layers.

- **Difference**: The difference between the base and blend pixels is used as the blend in the Difference Blending Modes. The colors of the base layer are reversed by white. It produces the same outcome as pressing Ctrl I (Windows) or Command I to invert the colors of the base layer (macOS).
  Dark grays slightly darken the image whereas black produces no change. For aligning layers with related information, this blending mode might be of great assistance. The outcome will become dark if two pixels are identical.
  Keyboard Shortcut: Alt Shift E (Windows) or Option Shift E (macOS)
  Neutral Colors: Black
  * Not available in the Lab Color Space.
- **Exclusion**: Exclusion and Difference are extremely similar. While blending with black results in no change, blending with white flips the values of the base colors. On the other hand, blending with 50% gray results in 50% gray.
  Keyboard Shortcut: Alt Shift X (Windows) or Option Shift X (macOS)
  Neutral Colors: Black
  * Not available in the Lab Color Space or 32-Bit Mode.
- **Subtract**: The base layer's pixel values are subtracted when using the Subtract Blending Mode. By reducing brightness, this Blending Mode severely darkens pixels.
  White has no impact. The outcome only becomes darker as the blend values increase brighter. Observe how the gradient's light portions are nearly pure black, whereas its dark areas just slightly changed. The results of Subtract and Divide are the exact opposite.

Keyboard Shortcut: None
Neutral Colors: Black
* Not available in the Lab Color Space.

✦ **Divide**: Divide converts each color into a percentage. White emerges from blending with the same color since any number divided by itself equals 1, or 100%. Due to the indefinite nature of diving by zero, black (0%) gives you black. Nothing changes. Divide has the exact opposite result as subtract.

White does nothing. The result only becomes brighter as the blend values go darker. While the light portions of the blend layer make a relatively tiny change, the dark areas of the blend layer produce brilliant hues. Divide produces the same outcome as flipping the Blend layer and selecting Color Dodge as the Blend Mode.
Keyboard Shortcut: None
Neutral Colors: White
* Not available in the Lab Color Space.

Component Blending Modes

The hue, saturation, and brightness of the primary color components are combined in the component blending modes to produce the mix.

The component group's Blend Modes are not available in the Grayscale Mode.

✦ **Hue**: The basic colors' brightness and saturation are preserved while the hue of the blend colors is kept.

If the neutral gray base layer, hue won't make a difference. With the Hue Blend Mode, a layer's colors could be altered while the original's tones and saturation were kept.
Keyboard Shortcut: Alt Shift U (Windows) or Option Shift U (macOS)
Neutral Colors: None
* Not available in the Grayscale Mode.

✦ **Saturation**: The hue and luminosity of the base colors are affected by the saturation of the blend colors in the saturation blending mode (details). If the base layer is a neutral gray, saturation won't make a difference.

Because none of the pixels contain saturation, a black-and-white blend layer will make the image black and white.
Keyboard Shortcut: Alt Shift T (Windows) or Option Shift T (macOS)
Neutral Colors: None
* Not available in Grayscale Mode.

✦ **Color**: The base colors' brightness (details) are affected by the hue and saturation of the blend colors when using the Color Blending Mode.

For coloring monochromatic photographs, the Color Blending Mode works well.

The second set of computed blending modes is color and luminance. You will receive the same outcome if you apply the Luminosity Blending Mode on the base layer, then reverse the order of the layers, as you will if you apply the Color Blending Mode to the blend layer.
Keyboard Shortcut: Alt Shift C (Windows) or Option Shift C (macOS)
Neutral Colors: None
* Not available in Grayscale Mode.

⬍ **Luminosity**: The hue and saturation of the base color are altered by the brightness (detail) of the mixed colors.

The second set of computed blending modes is luminance and color.
Keyboard Shortcut: Alt Shift Y (Windows) or Option Shift Y (macOS)
Neutral Colors: None
* Not available in Grayscale Mode.

Spicing up your Designs with Layer Styles

A **layer style** is a combination of two or more layer effects that are combined produce a more comprehensive appearance. The blend mode of the layer, together with its current Opacity and Fill Opacity settings, are also included in layer styles. Layer styles also include any Blending Options applied to the layer. **Layer effects** are the specific effects themselves, such as Drop Shadow, Stroke, Outer Glow, and so on. Layer effects and layer styles are frequently used interchangeably.

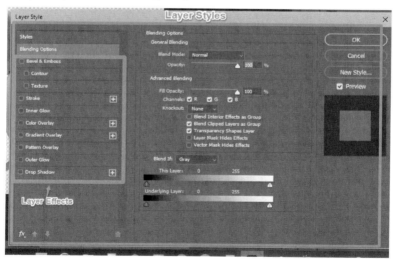

Use either of these methods to access the layer style`s window

136

- You may access the Layer Style dialog box by selecting **Blending Options** from the context menu when you right-click on your layer.

- You may access the Layer Style window by double-clicking on the thumbnail preview of your layer in the Layers Panel.

- From the **Menu Bar**, Select **Layer Style**.

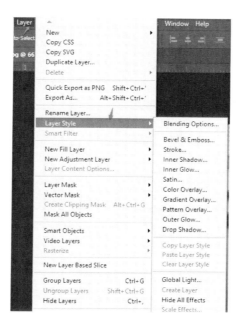

Lastly, you may want to access your layer-style dialog window from your layer panel by clicking on the layer effects icon (*fx*)

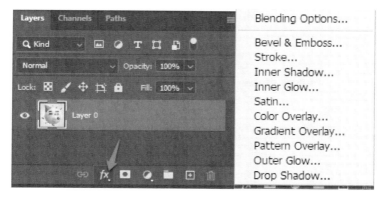

Preset Styles

Preset styles are layer styles that are ready-made layer styles made available in Photoshop. Simply click on a layer style to select it, and your layer will receive the effect right away.

To access the preset styles in Photoshop, follow either of these procedures.

138

✦ From the **Windows Menu** in the **Menu Bar**, Select **Styles**, and the style panel pops up afterward.

✦ You may also access them from the **layer styles dialog window**

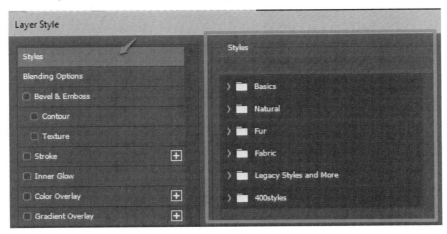

Layer Effects

In Photoshop, there is a group of non-destructive, customizable effects called layer effects that can be used on practically any type of layer. Even though there are ten various layer effects available, they may be divided into three basic categories: **Shadows** and **Glows**, **Overlays**, and **Strokes**. Layer effects are live effects that link directly to the layers they are applied on. Therefore, any effects that have been applied to a layer will immediately update if you change the contents of that layer.

Layer effects can be used with texts, images, and vector shapes to add realism or originality in ways that would be challenging, if not impossible, without layer effects.

Without permanently altering your image, you can apply several effects to a single layer, turn them on and off, tweak their parameters, and erase layer effects. To apply the same effects to numerous layers at once, you may even add layer effects to an entire layer group. Additionally, you can create incredible text effects by combining layer effects with type while keeping your text fully editable.

Below are the layer effects in Photoshop

- **Bevel & Emboss**: This layer effect makes your layer appear "popped out" or "pressed in" by applying both highlights and shadows.

- **Stroke**: The Stroke effect will use your chosen color, pattern, or gradient to outline your whole layer.

- **Inner Shadow**: The Inner Shadow effect adds a shadow to your layer's inner edges, giving them a recessed appearance.

✦ **Inner Glow**: The inner boundaries of your layer will be illuminated with the Inner Glow effect.

✦ **Satin**: Utilizing internal shading, the satin effect gives your layer a glossy appearance. For generating effects like fabric and glass, use this effect.

✦ **Color Overlay**: Any color you choose will fill your layer when using the Color Overlay effect. Both subtle and drastic color changes can be achieved using this technique.

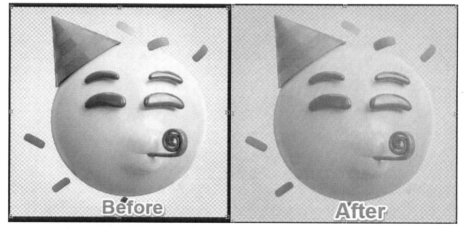

✦ **Gradient Overlay**: With the Gradient Overlay effect, at least two colors of your choice will be filled into your layer and seamlessly blended.

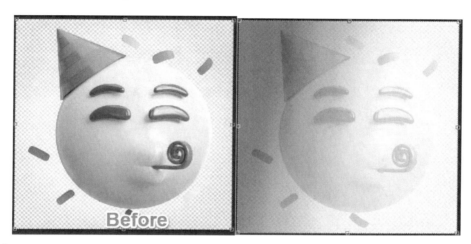

❖ **Pattern Overlay**: Your layer will be filled with the pattern of your choice if you use the Pattern Overlay effect.

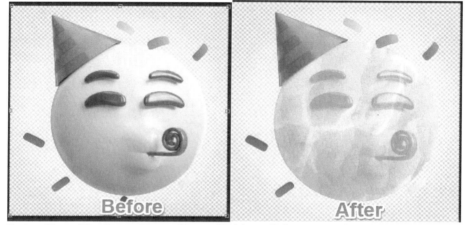

❖ **Outer Glow**: The Outer Glow effect will shine a light on your layer's outer edge.

❖ **Drop Shadow**: The shadow behind your layer will be added using the drop shadow effect.

Shadow

CHAPTER SIX

SELECTING AND MASKING

What you will learn in this chapter.

- **How to make selections in Photoshop.**
- **How to use the various selection tools in Photoshop.**
- **How to mask a portion of selection.**
- **How to refine a selected portion in Photoshop.**

Starting with Selection and Selection Tools

A selection is a portion of a picture that you pick out. The area is modifiable when you make a selection (for example, you can lighten one part of a photo without affecting the rest). A selection can be created using a **selection command** or a **selection tool**. The selection is encircled by a selection border that can be hidden. Pixels inside the selection border can be modified, copied, or deleted, but until the selection is deselected, you are unable to interact with any areas outside the selection border.

For various selections, Adobe Photoshop offers selection tools. For instance, the Elliptical Marquee tool selects elliptical and circular areas, and the Magic Wand tool allows for a one-click selection of an area with related colors. One of the Lasso tools can be used to make more intricate selections. With feathering and anti-aliasing, you can even soften a selection's edges. Except for the marquee tools, every other selection tool works effectively based on the Color Algorithm.

We'll examine twelve of Photoshop's most crucial selection tools in this section. We'll go over each command and each tool's functions and offer some advice on how to utilize them efficiently.

Many of Photoshop's selection tools are nested with related tools on the toolbar. The Tools panel, which is by default on the left side of your screen, contains the selection tools.

The three nests of selection tools present in the Tool Bar are **The Marquee Tools**, **The Lasso Tools,** and **The Object Selection Tools**.

The Marquee Tools

The Marquee Tools nest are **Rectangular Marquee Tool**, **Elliptical Marquee Tool**, **Single Row Marquee Tool**, and **Single Column Marquee Tool**.

You can select a shape by dragging it over an area with the Marquee tools. You have the option of using two single-line forms, an elliptical marquee tool, or a rectangular marquee tool. Select the marquee you wish to use, then click and drag the shape to the appropriate size. When you let go of it, the choice is displayed. When dragging to make a square or circle, hold the Shift key, you drag the shape by default from a corner by doing this. To draw a shape that starts in the center, hold down the **Alt key(Windows)** or **Option key(macOS).**

You can switch the style from Normal to Fixed Ratio in the **Options Bar**. As a result, a square or circle is formed. You may also select a fixed size (a selection of a predetermined size).

Additional options are displayed in the **Options Bar** when you select a selection tool. These Options come with a collection of icons that show how different choices will interact with one another.

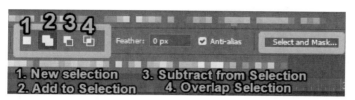

- A Square ▣ (New Selection) allows you to draw a new selection

- The Overlapping Squares ▣ (Add to Selection) allows you to add to previous selections

- A filled and an empty square ▣ (Subtract from selection): allows you to remove the new selection from the previous one. Another way to use this feature is to hold the Alt Key (Windows) or Option Key (macOS) while making a new selection.

- The Second Overlapping Square (Overlap Selection): allows you to keep the area shared by the new and previous selections.

Other options in the Options Bar Include;

- Feather: This creates a smooth transition between the selection and its surroundings
- Select and Mask: Using your selection, the Select and Mask button will generate a masking layer. Shortcut = Alt key + Ctrl R(Windows) and Option Key + Cmd R(macOS)

Note: that some of these features are available in all of the selection tools.

The Lasso Tools
The Lasso Tools nests three other selection tools and they are **Lasso Tool, Polygonal Lasso tool,** and **Magnetic Lasso Tool.**

- **Lasso Tool**: You can draw a free-form lasso around an object to choose it using this tool. The device is not particularly accurate. When you want to make a broad choice, use it.
- **Polygonal Lasso Tool**: The Polygonal Lasso chooses geometric forms with only straight lines. These might not just be squares or rectangles, but also more intricate shapes. To make a line, click and drag along a shape's edge. Just one click will turn a corner. The tool stops the line there and allows you to modify the direction. After that, drag to create a horizontal or vertical line while holding down the Shift key. When you double-click or go back to where you started, the selected shape is finished.
- **Magnetic Lasso Tool**: The Magnetic Lasso tool functions similarly to the Lasso. To choose an object, Firstly, draw around it. To make a more accurate decision as you draw, the line is drawn to edges like a magnet. When an item has several curves, this tool works effectively for you.

  The object you want to choose should have a clickable edge. Drag the line around the shape after that. When a tool locks onto an edge, pins start to appear. When you double-click or click where you first clicked, the selection shape is finished.

  The magnetic tool resembles a circle. If you activate Caps Lock, you can see this more clearly. Photoshop searches the inside of the circle for a border. expanding the width in the options bar makes the circle bigger. Additionally, you can change the contrast to help the algorithm locate an advantage. The quantity of pins positioned along the edge is called frequency. If you wish to see more or fewer pins, adjust this. But at any point along the line, you can click to add a pin.

Object Selection Tools

In this tool nest are **Object Selection, Quick Selection Tool,** and **Magic Wand Tool**.

✛ **Object Selection**: was added by Adobe to Photoshop in 2019. It initially has the same appearance as the Marquee tool. To choose an object, first, draw a rectangle or lasso around it. Photoshop then examines the shape's contents to identify any objects therein. The selection is then further refined by the program around the subject.

✛ **Quick Selection**: A quick method for choosing a clearly defined object is to use the Quick Selection tool. To choose an object, click inside of it. Photoshop looks for boundaries and colors before enlarging the selection to include related pixels. Click on another part of the object to add to the selection. Alternatively, paint in the selection using the cursor.

Similar to a brush tool, the Quick Selection tool operates. The brush stroke's size, hardness, spacing, and angle are all adjustable. To add to the selection, click the Plus icon. To remove a portion of the selection, click the minus sign or hold down the choice key.

✛ **Magic Wand**: The Magic Wand tool should be used to choose colors. Any color in your image can be clicked to highlight all of its occurrences in the image.

The degree of precision in the color selection is altered by **Tolerance** in the Options bar.

The selection of colors is exact at low tolerance levels. The algorithm chooses colors similar to the one you chose when the tolerance is larger. To increase the selection, click a second color. To remove a color from the selection, click it while holding down the option key.

Colors are chosen for the entire frame if the **Contiguous box** is left unticked. By using the Contiguous checkbox, only colors close to the one chosen are available. Colors are chosen for the entire frame if the Contiguous box is left unticked. By using the Contiguous checkbox, only colors close to the one chosen are available.

Not all the selection tools available in Photoshop are kept in the Tool Bar, Photoshop has a **Select Menu** in the **Menu Bar**. Selection tools are some of the options. Others modify the selection tools nested in the Tool Bar

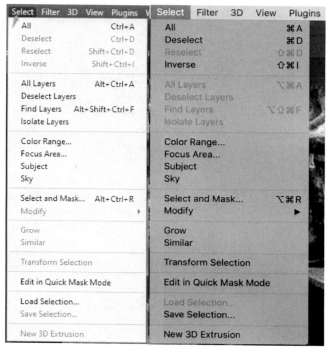

✦ **All**: this is a command that allows you to select all parts of a layer. Shortcut =Ctrl/Cmd + A

✦ **Deselect**: this is a command that permits you to deselect every selection in a layer. Shortcuts = Ctrl/Cmd D

✦ **Reselect: this** is a command that allows you to reselect previous selections. Shortcut = Shift+ Ctrl/Cmd + D

✦ **Inverse:** this command allows you to inverse your selection, that is, it deselects your original selection and selects the parts that are outside your selection. Shortcut = Shift + Ctrl/Cmd + I

Other Selection tools in the Select Menu are: **Select Subject**, **Select Sky**, **Color Range**, **Focus Area**, and **Select and Mask**.

Select Object

Similar to the Object Selection tool is the Select Subject tool. But using it is simpler. . Photoshop analyzes your image and picks up potential subjects. This selection tool does not always make perfect selections, so in cases when your selections aren`t perfect, you can refine your selection using another tool like the lasso tools. To access **the Select Subject** feature,

- Click on **Select** in the **Menu Bar**
- From the Select drop-down menu click on **Subject**

Another way to access the Select Subject feature is to access it from the **Object Selection Tools`** Options Bar.

Select Sky

Prior to Adobe including a Sky Replacement tool in Photoshop, sky had to be manually masked. This selecting tool made the task simpler Photoshop can recognize the sky even when there are distractions, like green trees.

To access this selection tool,

- Click on **Select** in the **Menu Bar**
- Select **Sky** in the **Select** drop-down menu.

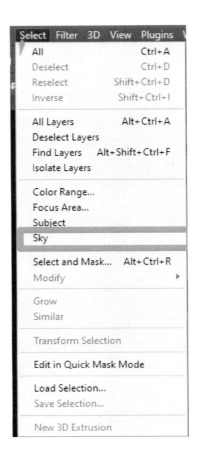

Color Range

The Color Range tool can function similarly to the Magic Wand tool.

To use the color range selection tool effectively, follow the procedure below:

- ☀ Open the image you want to select from in photoshop
- ☀ Use Ctrl/Cmd +A to select your entire image.
- ☀ From the **Menu Bar**, click on **Select**
- ☀ In the **Select`s** drop-down menu, select **Color Range.**
- ☀ The window changes. From the drop-down option,

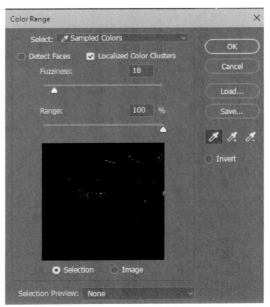

o **Select:** The Select option is located right at the top of the dialog box. It is set to Sampled Colors by default:

What we choose to select in the image is controlled by the Select option. When the option for Sampled Colors is selected, the Color Range command functions similarly to the Magic Wand.

A list of the various selection alternatives will appear when you click on the phrase "**Sampled Colors**," allowing you to make your decision. For instance, by selecting a certain color from the list, we may instantaneously choose all the pixels that are that color (reds, yellows, blues, etc.). Alternately, we can choose **Highlights** or **Shadows** to quickly identify the image's brightest or darkest pixels, respectively, or the **Mid-tones** to identify the part of the image that is between the brightest and darkest pixels. The **Skin Tones** allows you to select colos that resemble common skin tones. Leave the option set to Sampled Colors, which is what we'll be focused on, these extra options can be useful in specific circumstances

- ○ **The Eye Dropper Tool**: We use an eyedropper tool to select the image with Color Range. In fact, Color Range provides us with three eyedropper tools: one for initial selection , one for adding to the selection , and one for removing from the selection . These tools are located on the right side of the dialog box.

- ○ **The Selection Preview Window**: The selection preview window, which is located in the bottom part of the dialog box, allows us to get a live preview of the area(s) of the image that we have picked by using the eyedroppers. Our choice is shown in the preview box as a grayscale picture. The preview window operates exactly the same way as layer masks do. The preview window will display the fully selected portions of the image as white and the unselected portions as black.

Select the Selection Preview option to see the selection in the image window.

None Displays the first picture.

Grayscale Displays black for pixels that are not selected, gray for ones that are partially selected, and white for those that are fully selected.

Black Matte Displays the original image for pixels that have been chosen and black for those that have not. Bright pictures go well with this selection.

When using a **white matte**, selected pixels display the original image while unselected pixels display white. Dark photos work well with this choice.

In the **Quick Mask** Options dialog box, you can choose a custom color to overlay unselected areas in place of the original image.

- Fuzziness: Just like **Tolerance** works in the **Magic Wand Tool**, so does **Fuzziness** in **Color Range.** The selection's color range is controlled by the Fuzziness parameter, which also affects how many pixels are partially picked (gray areas in the selection preview). To limit the color range, set a low Fuzziness value; to widen the range, set a high value.

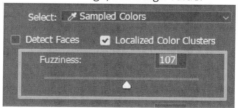

- **Detect Face**: This feature work with the skin tones option for accurate skin tone selection.

o **Localized Color Clusters & Range**: As soon as we turn on Localized Color Clusters, another option, Range, becomes available directly below the Fuzziness slider.

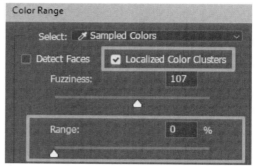

Use the Range slider to adjust how distant or close a color must be to the sample points in order for it to be included in the selection if you selected Localized Color Clusters. Photoshop will search the entire image for patches of matching color to add to our selection when Range is set to 100% (or when the Localized Color Clusters option is disabled). However, by moving the slider to the left and lowering the Range value, we instruct Photoshop to focus solely on portions of the image that are close to where we clicked and to ignore those that are too far away.

o **Invert**: This tool is located just below the eye dropper tool in the color range preview window. As the name implies, it is used to invert selections.

o After you're done with making adjustments to your selections, then Click **Ok** to close out the Color Range preview window.

Focus Area

Photoshop can now analyze an image, determine what is in focus and what is not, and then make a selection of just the area we need if we need to isolate a person or subject from the background and that person or subject happens to be in focus (within the depth of field) while the background is blurred and out of focus. This is possible because of the Focus Area selection tools.

To use the Focus Area selection tool effectively, follow the procedure below:

- In the **Select**'s drop-down menu from the **Menu Bar**, Select **Focus Area.**
- The Focus Area window pops up,

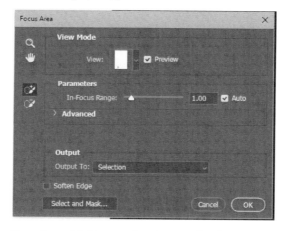

- Photoshop will make a highly precise Auto selection as it searches for in focus components. The selection can be made larger or smaller by dragging the In-**Focus Range slider** in the Parameters box. Try different things until you find a good basic choice.

⬍ Set the **View Mode** to your preference and note that the **Hand** and **Zoom tool** are options are available for quick access if you need them. The **Preview option** allows you to check the changes you have made to your image

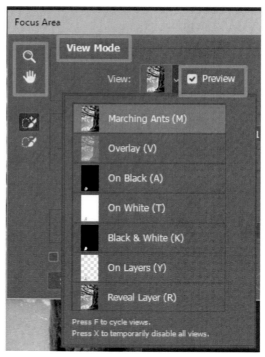

✦ The **Image Noise Level slider** is located in the **Advanced section**. To change the Focus Area's sensitivity to image noise, move the slider to the left or right.

✦ Once you've improved upon the initial selection as much as possible with the In-Focus Range slider (as well as the Image Noise Level slider), It's time to exert more manual control over the selection using two potent brush tools, the **Focus Area Add Tool** and the **Focus Area Subtract Tool.** By selecting their icons on the left side of the Focus Area dialog box, we can access them. By default, the Focus Area Add Tool (the one at the top with the plus sign in the icon) is chosen:

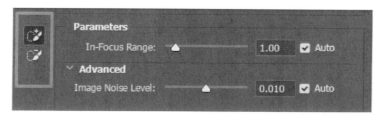

Quick Tip: On the keyboard, hitting the letter **E** will switch between the Focus Area Add and Focus Area Select tools.

- By choosing the **Soften Edges option** in the dialog box's lower left, you can smooth out the edges of your image.

- If you're satisfied with your choice so far, you may select from a variety of output kinds using the **Output To** option located near the bottom of the Focus Area dialog box. The list of choices is opened by clicking the output type box. We can create it as a new layer, a layer mask, or the conventional "marching ants" selection outline, among other output formats:

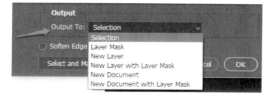

- Once you are done with making your selection, Click **Ok**

Using The Quick Mask Mode
The Quick Mask Mode is a very simple way of making selection in Photoshop.

To use the Quick Mask Mode follow the procedures below,

- You can open the Quick Mask Mode either of the following ways;
  - Click the icon found at the bottom of the toolbar.

o Additionally, you can open a Quick Mask by selecting **Select** > **Edit in Quick Mask** from the Select drop-down menu.

- On the Keyboard, click The **Q** key and it opens you up to the Quick Mask Mode automatically.
❖ The areas that are not selected while in this mode will be covered by a red color overlay, while the selected pixels will be left exposed.

❖ Paint over with white Brush to add to the mask or black brush to deduct from it (your strokes will appear as a red overlay). Grayscale brush can also be used to create semi-transparent choices.

❖ To change the mask's color and opacity, double click on it. Additionally, you have the option to have the mask display the selected regions rather than the unselected regions. To see marching ants encircling the selected area, click the **icon** or **Q** once more.

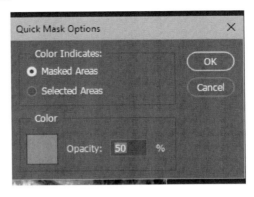

Selecting and Masking

As their name suggests, the selection tools discussed above are used to pick certain objects or areas of images. You have the option to remove or alter your selections. Masking your selection is the easiest approach to remove a portion of it without ruining the original image.

As previously mentioned, you can choose a portion of an image using the selection tools, but you can isolate the chosen area using masking. Other portions of an image that aren't chosen during selection can be removed with the use of masking. But because it is unbreakable, any changes made to an image via masking are not irreversible. By deleting or turning off the layer mask, you can quickly undo the modifications you made. The layer mask makes masking unbreakable.

The Select and Mask Options

This feature is also a selection option in Photoshop. It allows you to select and mask your selections. Embedded in this option are advanced features that permit you to refine your selections to your satisfaction. The Select and Mask Window is also accessible by other selection tools for further edits of the image.

You can access the select and mask option either of the following ways,

- ✦ From the **Options Bar** of the **Object Selection tools**, **Quick Selection tools** and the **Lasso tools.**

+ Ultimately, you can access the select and mask option from the **Select** drop-down menu from the **Menu bar.**

To use the Select and Mask option, follow the procedure below:

+ After making your selection with any of the selection tools, access the selection and mask option from either of the following ways above.
+ The select and mask option becomes enabled,

○ **Quick Selection Tool**: Don't be surprised that a quick selection tool is also available in the select and mask window, this tool functions like the typical quick selection tool.

When you click or click-drag the area you want to select, make a rapid selection based on similarity in color and texture. The Quick Selection tool automatically and logically produces a border, so the selection you make doesn't need to be exact.

○ **Refine Edge Brush Tool:** Use this tool to adjust the boundary region where edge refinement takes place precisely. For example, to add small details to the selection, brush over soft parts like hair or fur. To change the brush size, press the bracket keys.

163

o **Brush Tool**: Use the Quick Selection tool (or another selection tool) to create a crude selection, and then use the Refine Edge Brush tool to make it more precise. Use the Brush tool to clean up or complete details now.

Use the Brush tool to fine-tune a selection, in either Add mode to paint over the region you want to pick or Subtract mode to paint over the area you don't want to select.

o **Object Selection Tool**: Around an object, draw a lasso or a rectangular area. The object is located and automatically selected using the Object Selection tool inside the specified zone.

o **Lasso Tool**: Make selection borders by hand. You can choose exactly what you want by using this tool.

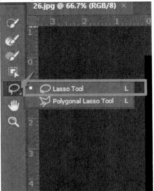

o **Polygonal Lasso Tool**: Draw portions of a selection border with straight edges. You can use this tool to make precise or arbitrary selections. When you right-click the Lasso Tool, you can choose this tool from the available selections.

o **Hand Tool**: Navigate around an image document quickly. Drag this tool around the picture canvas after selecting it. Holding down the spacebar while using any other tool allows you to swiftly switch to the Hand tool.

o **Zoom Tool**: Magnify the image and move around it.

○ **Option Bars**: The Options Bar carries the extra information of a tool. The image below is the options bar for the quick selection tool.

Other options available in the options bar are below,

⬍ **Add** or **Subtract**: The refining area may be increased or decreased. Adjust the brush size if necessary.

⬍ **Sample All Layers:** creates a selection based on all layers, as opposed to only the one that is currently selected.

⬍ **Select Subject:** Select the main subjects in a photo in a single click.

⬍ **Refine Hair:** Find and improve challenging hair selections with just one click. For the best outcomes, combine with Object Aware.

Refine the Selection

In this section, we continue to explore the Select and Mask Workspace. In the Select and Mask workspace's Properties panel, you can fine-tune your selection. Adjust the following settings to do this:

• **View Mode**: Choose one of the following view modes for your selection from the View pop-up menu:

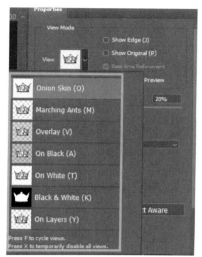

- o **Onion Skin (O)**: visualizes the choice as an animated onion skin scheme
- o **Marching Ants (M):** the selection's borders as marching ants.
- o **Overlay (V)**: visualizes the selection as a transparent color. Areas that are not selected are shown in that color. The standard shade is red.
- o **On Black (A)**: places the selection over a black background when you pick this option.
- o **On White (T)**: positions the selected area against a white background.
- o **Black & White (K)**: Creates a black and white mask out of the selection.
- o **On Layers (Y):** surrounds the selection with areas of transparency.

Press **F** to switch between the modes, then **X** to turn off each option for a while.

- o **Show Edge**: Shows the area of refinement.
- o **Show original**: Shows the original selection.

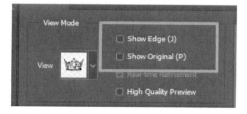

- o **High Quality Preview**: This renders an accurate change preview. Performance may be impacted by this choice. Hold down the left mouse button (mouse down) while manipulating the image with this option

168

selected to see a higher-resolution preview. When this option is deselected, even when the mouse is down, a lower-resolution preview is shown.

- o **Transparency/Opacity**: Transparency and opacity are set for **the View Mode.**
- **Refine Modes**: Color Aware and Object Aware modes are the two modes present in this setting section.
  - o **Color Aware**: Choose this mode for simple or contrasting backgrounds.
  - o **Object Aware**: Select this mode if the background has intricate hair or fur.

- **Edge Detection Settings**:
  - o Radius: This parameter establishes the size of the selection border where edge refinement takes place. For sharp edges, use a small radius; for softer edges, a larger radius
  - o Smart Radius: Provides a refinement zone around the edge of your selection with a changeable width. This option is advantageous, among other uses, if the portrait you choose has both shoulders and hair. The hair in such images could need more finessing than the shoulders, where the edge is more uniform.

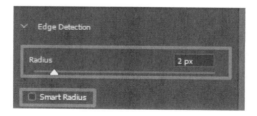

169

- **Global Refinement Settings**:
  - o **Smooth**: Smoothens the selection border's rough edges (such as "hills and valleys") to give it a more even appearance.
  - o **Feather**: Softens the boundary between the selected area and the pixels around it.
  - o **Contrast**: Soft-edged transitions along the selection border become more abrupt as they are magnified. The Smart Radius option and refining tools are frequently more efficient.
  - o **Shift Edge**: Shifts soft-edged borders inward when the value is negative or outward when the value is positive. It may be possible to get rid of undesirable backdrop colors from selection edges by moving these borders inward.

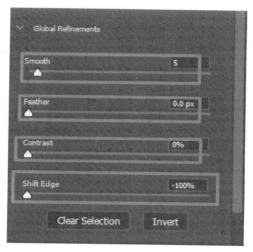

- **Output Settings**:
  - o **Decontaminate Colors**: This setting's option replaces color fringes with the color of neighboring fully picked pixels to decontaminate colors. The softness of the selection margins is inversely correlated with the strength of color replacement. To alter the degree of decontamination, move the slider. The default setting is 100% (the maximum strength). This option necessitates export to a new layer or document because it modifies the pixel color. Keep the initial layer so you may go back to it if necessary.
  - o **Output To**: specifies whether the refined selection creates a selection or mask on the current layer, creates a new layer, or creates a new document as the output.

170

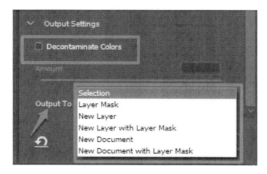

Additional information to take note:

✦ To return the settings to the ones you saw when you first opened the Select and Mask workspace, click 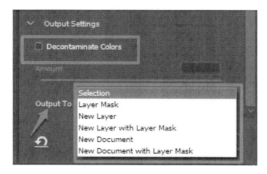 (**Reset The Workspace**). Additionally, choosing this option restores the image's initial selections and masks from when you first opened the Select and Mask workspace.

To preserve the settings for use with subsequent photos, select **Remember Settings**. If the current image is opened again in the **Select and Mask workspace**, the settings are applied again to all ensuing photos.

CHAPTER SEVEN

TYPOGRAPHY; THE TYPE TOOLS IN PHOTOSHOP

The basics of Typography

Typography is the practice of placing letters and text in a way that makes it simple for readers to read, comprehend, and find visually appealing.

In order to evoke specific emotions and convey specific messages, typeface appearance, style, and structure are all involved. Put another way, typography adds vibrancy to the writing.

There are different elements of Typography and most of them are found in the **Character Panel** in Photoshop too.

Some of the elements of typography are explained below. explained below;

- **Fonts and Typeface**: A font is a graphic representation of a text character, but a typeface is a design style that consists of a variety of characters in different sizes and weights.
  A typeface is essentially a group of linked fonts, and by fonts we mean the many weights, widths, and styles that make up a typeface.

172

There are three basic kinds of typeface: **Serif**, **Sans-Serif**, and **Script** typefaces are the three fundamental types.

- ○ **Serif**: The extra markings at the end of each letter make a typeface a serif. Serif fonts provide an air of heritage, history, authority, and integrity thanks to the presence of these little strokes and components.
- ○ **Sans-Serif**: Sans-serif typefaces are identified by what they do not have, as suggested by their name. The sans-serif font family is considered to be considerably more contemporary and bold because it lacks the more conventional strokes and dashes of serif. Because of this, it is easy to read and, when used in headlines, it attracts attention more effectively than serifs.
- ○ **Scripts**: This typeface's purpose is more aesthetically pleasing than intelligible, as its name once more indicates. Therefore, these are far more frequently employed in brand names, logos, and short titles.

- ✦ **Color**: One of the most fascinating aspects of typography is color. Here is where interface designers may really express their creativity and take the design to the next level.

Text color, though, should not be taken lightly; done right, it may make the text pop out and express the message's tone.

The three main elements of color are value, hue, and saturation.

Even for individuals with visual impairments, a smart designer can balance these three elements to create appealing and easily readable writing be able to balance these three elements to create writing that is appealing and easily readable.

Designers frequently check this by examining the text in greyscale (without color) and making adjustments if the text contrasts with the background color too darkly or too brightly.

✦ **Font Size**: The size of any font you are using is determined by the purpose of the text in the design. You can determine the hierarchy in a design by sizing your texts according to their importance.

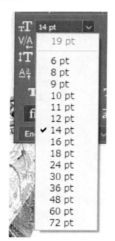

✦ **Leading**: Leading is the space between lines of text.

- **Kerning**: Adjusting the distance between individual characters is a process known as kerneling.

  Kerning aims to create more evenly distributed type by balancing the appearance of whitespace between characters. It's crucial to remember this while using huge typography and headers. When aiming to avoid line breaks in your design, kerning can be very useful even though it is less crucial in paragraphs of small type.

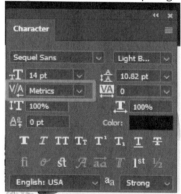

- **Whitespace**: The empty area in a composition is known as white space or negative space.

  Your text will be challenging to read if your font and other design components are crowded and placed too closely together. Whitespace is useful in this situation.
- **Hierarchy**: One of the most important typographic principles is hierarchy. Typographic hierarchy seeks to establish a significant separation between important textual elements that should be noticed and read first and ordinary textual elements.

Using Texts in Photoshop

The Type tool allows you to add text to your file. Adding text to photographs to make a poster, holiday card, or invitation is just one example of how you may utilize it in a variety of projects. Additionally, you can change the text to suit your requirements.

The Type tool is located in the Toolbar. Nested in the type tools are other variants of type tools and they are **Horizontal Type Tool**, **Vertical Type Tool**, **Horizontal Type Mask Tool**, and **Vertical Type Mask Tool.**

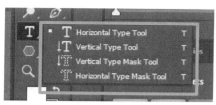

- ♦ **The horizontal type tool** is your standard typing instrument. You may make simple text on a horizontal plane using it.
- ♦ You can generate basic text that is created on a vertical plane using **the Vertical Type Tool** (from top to bottom).
- ♦ **Horizontal Type Mask Tool** - Rather of displaying live text, this tool generates a selection of the text. Following that, the selections can be utilized to make masks and clips.
- ♦ Instead of displaying live text, **the vertical type mask tool** generates a selection of the text. A vertical plane will be used to format the text. Following that, the selections can be utilized to make masks and clips.

The Character Panel and The Paragraph panel

When using types or editing texts in Photoshop, you use either the **Options Bar** or the **Character Panel** and the **Paragraph Panel**. One advantage of these two tools is that they provide you more options than the Option Bar. These two panels are crucial to using to type tool effectively. The Character Panel displays every option needed to edit your type effectively while The Paragraph Panel displays the alignment options for your type. When working with paragraphs or large blocks of text, the Paragraph Palette comes in quite handy. Options such word hyphenation, indentation, and alignment can all be found in the Paragraph panel.

The Options Bar

The Character Panel

The Paragraph Panel

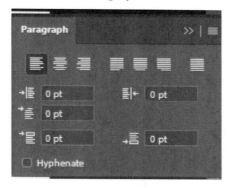

The options below are made available by either of the three panels above are;

- **Font Family**: Any font on your system is available for selection. The Add Fonts dialog box can be used to install a font if the one you want to use isn't already on your computer. This option is present in both the Options bar and Character panel

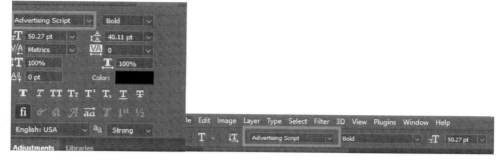

✦ **Font Style**: Regular, italic, bold, and bold italic are your options. This option is present in both the Options bar and Character panel

✦ **Font Size**: Either a numerical value or a selection of predetermined sizes can be entered. This option is present in both the Options bar and Character panel

✦ **Leading**: This is the distance that exists between text lines. A range of pre-set numbers is available, or you can specify a numeric value.

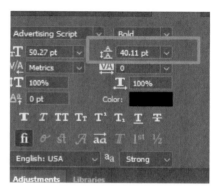

✦ **Tracking**: This option is how much space there is between each character in a piece of text.

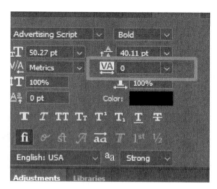

✦ **Kerning**: The distance between two particular letters or characters is controlled by the kerning. Kerning and tracking are frequently confused with one another since they appear to be similar yet differ significantly. Tracking determines the distance between a variety of characters, while kerning regulates the distance between two particular characters.

- ❖ **Vertical and Horizontal Scale**: The Vertical Scale (left) and Horizontal Scale (right) settings are located in the Character panel behind the Kerning and Tracking options. Type can be scaled either vertically or horizontally using these settings.

- ❖ **Baseline Shift**: is the space between characters you move above or below the baseline

- ❖ **Anti-aliasing**: To maintain the appearance of smooth letter edges, anti-aliasing is applied. Without anti-aliasing, the majority of letters would have blocky, jagged edges. This option is present in both the Options bar and Character panel

- ❖ **Text Color**: To choose any color from the Color Picker, simply click the color swatch. By selecting a hue and then indicating how light or dark you want it to be, you may also generate "tints." Tints are particularly effective for producing minor color differences, such as several hues of gray. This option is present in both the Options bar and Character panel

✦ **Faux Bold**: This option allows you to bolden a type when the font you are using does not include them.

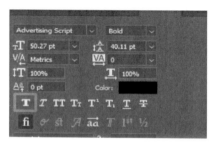

✦ **Faux italic**. This option allows you to apply the italics effect to your texts.

✦ **All Caps**: This option converts all your texts into uppercase letters when checked.

✦ **Small Caps**: This allows you to convert all your texts into lowercase letters

✦ **Superscript and Subscript**: Reduced-size text that is raised or lowered in proportion to the baseline of a typeface is referred to as superscript and subscript text (also known as superior and inferior text).

✦ **Underline and Strikethrough**: The Underline option allows you to underline a text while Strikethrough creates a line that cuts through your selected texts.

✦ **Language Selection**: The Language Selection box is located in the bottom left corner of the Character panel. Unfortunately, this function is not intended to translate our content from one language to another, despite the fact that it would

be amazing if Photoshop could do so. Simply to ensure that you're using the proper spelling and hyphenation for whichever language you have selected.

The Options below are available in the Paragraph Panel.

- ✦ **The Alignment Options**: There is a row of icons for aligning and justifying our text across the top of the paragraph panel. The alignment options are represented by the first three icons in the row on the left. **Left Align Text**, **Center Text**, and **Right Align Text** are shown in that order. These three alignment options are the only paragraph options also present in the Options Bar

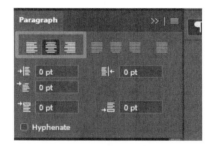

- ✦ **The Justification Options**: The options for justification are the next four icons in the row towards the top of the paragraph panel. **Justify Last Left**, **Justify Last Centered**, **Justify Last Right**, and **lastly Justify** All are listed from left to right. These choices are restricted to the Paragraph panel. In fact, the Paragraph panel is the only place where we'll look at the possibilities moving forward. Only the alignment options we just looked at above are available here as well as in the Options Bar.

  Any of these justification options causes Photoshop to resize the word spacing such that every line of text in the paragraph covers the text box's width from left to right, forming a "block" of text. The sole distinction between the four alternatives is how Photoshop treats the paragraph's very last line.

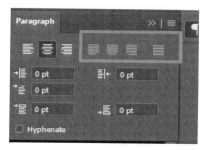

✦ **The Indent options**: Three indent options are available underneath the alignment and justification icons: **Indent Left Margin (top left), Indent Right Margin (top right)**, and **Indent First Line (bottom left)**. By default, all three are set to 0 points:

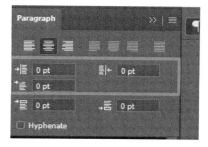

With the help of these options, we may put space between the full paragraph and the left or right sides of the text box or simply the first line. You can either click inside the input box and manually type a value to change any of the indent choices' values.

✦ **Paragraph Spacing Options**: The suitably called **Add Space Before Paragraph** (left) and **Add Space After Paragraph** (right) tools in Photoshop allow us to add space before or after a paragraph.

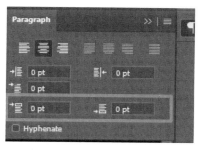

✦ **Hyphenate**: When utilizing any of the justification choices, hyphenation is very useful because it enables Photoshop to split lengthier sentences up onto different lines, making it simpler to space the words out in a way that is more aesthetically pleasing. However, you can simply uncheck the option to prevent hyphenation if you don't like it or just don't want to utilize it in a certain circumstance.

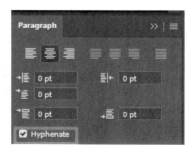

Other commands and more advanced features can be found in the Type Menu located at the Menu bar.

Working With Texts
To insert texts in a file,

- Open your file in Photoshop
- Choose the **Type tool** from the **toolbar**, or click 'T' to instantly choose it. By default, the tool that allows you to add text horizontally is selected. Click the Type tool once more to access the other type tool variants.
- Would you like to include a heading or a title? To type it, simply click anywhere on the canvas. Photoshop refers to this as point text or you drag your mouse cursor to create a bounding box to insert your text. This is used when you wish to type a paragraph.

- When you generate point or paragraph text, a type layer is automatically produced and is indicated in the **Layers panel** by the T icon.
- You can adjust your type settings in the **Options Bar**, The **Character Panel** or **Paragraph Panel**.
- Type your text. Click the options button or hit **Esc** to save your changes, and you're good to go!

To Select Text(s),

- Open the Photoshop document with the text you want to modify. Ensure that the text you want to edit must be on a type layer so that editing can be possible
- Pick the **Move tool** (⊕)from the toolbar and double-click the text you wish to select to select the full text or paragraph on a type layer.
- Simply choose the **Type tool** from the **toolbar**, click, and then drag the mouse over the characters you wish to pick to select one or more characters on a type layer.

To edit text(s),

- Open the Photoshop document that contains the desired text changes. To allow for editing, make sure the text you wish to change is on a type layer.
- From the **toolbar**, choose the **Type tool**.
- Choose the text that needs editing.
- You can change your font type, font size, font color, text alignment, and text style using the **Character Panel** or the **Options bar** at the top.
- To save your adjustments, click ☑ in the options bar at the end.

To Copy and Paste Text(s),

Before we begin this exercise, It is important to know that Text from other documents can be copied and pasted into your Photoshop project (PSD). from a Word document, a PDF, a web page, or another Photoshop file, for instance (PSD).

- To copy and paste from a non-photoshop file do the following,
  - To pick text in a non-Photoshop document, such as a Word document, PDF, or web page, simply click and drag the pointer over the text.
  - To copy the highlighted text, hit **Control+C** on a Windows computer or **Command+C** on a Mac.
  - Select the Type tool from the toolbar, then open the Photoshop document (PSD) where you wish to paste the copied text.
  - From the Layers panel, choose the type layer that you wish to paste the text into. If you don`t have a type layer, you can create a new one.

- To paste your text, select **Edit** > **Paste** or hit **Command+V** on a Mac or **Control+V** on a Windows computer. Select **Edit** > **Undo Paste Text** to undo.
- ✦ To copy and paste from another Photoshop document
  - To copy the text from a PSD, open the PSD.
  - Choose **Edit** > **Copy** after selecting the text you wish to copy, or you may just click **Command+C** (on Mac OS) or **Control+C** (on Windows).
  - Select a type layer in the PSD after opening it and pasting the text within. If you wish to add another type layer or don't have any type layers, you can simply do so by creating a new type layer.
  - To paste your text in the center of your canvas, select **Edit** > **Paste**. To paste the text exactly as it appeared in the PSD that you had copied, select **Edit** > **Paste Special** > **Paste in Place**.

To resize text(s),

- ✦ Open the Photoshop document that contains the desired text changes. To allow for editing, make sure the text you wish to change is on a type layer.
- ✦ Select the image you desire to resize and do either of the following;
  - Change the size of the texts in the **Character panel**.

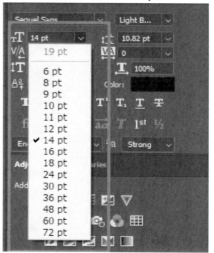

  - Change the size of the texts in the **Options bar**

  - Select on the type layer you desire to resize and click on the bounding box to resize it. Ensure that Show Transform Controls in checked in the **Options Bar**

187

- To save your adjustments, click ✅ in the options bar at the end.

To resize one or more characters on a type layer,

- Open the Photoshop document that contains the text you desire to make changes to. To allow for editing, make sure the text you wish to change is on a type layer.
- Select the type layer you want to make changes to and do either of the following;
  - Choose the 🔲font size option you desire in the **options bar**'s box or in the **Character Panel**. Real-time modifications are shown.
- You're finished after you click ✅ in the options bar! In the options bar, click 🚫 to undo your changes.

To move text(s),

- The Photoshop document with the text you want to modify should be opened. Make sure the text you want to update is on a type layer so that editing is possible.
- The text you want to transfer is on a type layer; choose that layer.
- In the **toolbar**, pick the **Move tool**.
- Select **Auto Select Layer** in the options bar, and then click the text you want to transfer.

- The black arrow will then allow you to see the transform box.
- To position the text where you desire, click and drag the transform box, then let go of it.

To change Color pf Text(s),

- The Photoshop document with the text you want to modify should be opened. Make sure the text you want to update is on a type layer so that editing is possible.
- Click the text whose color you want to change, then choose the **Type tool** from the **toolbar**. The type layer's whole text is selected.
- In the **Options bar** or in the **Character Panel**, select the **Color Picker (Text Color) icon.**

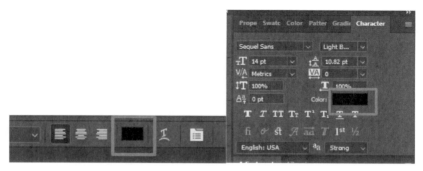

✦ Choose your color by adjusting the color slider as desired. As you choose several colors, you can instantly observe how your text color changes.

✦ Click **OK** after you're satisfied with the color of your text.

To align and justify Text(s),

✦ Open the Photoshop document containing the text you wish to edit. To allow for editing, ensure that the text you wish to change is on a type layer.

✦ From the Layers panel, choose the type layer that contains the paragraph you wish to justify.

✦ You may view the numerous Justify choices in the **Paragraph panel**. To see the changes as they happen, choose a choice.

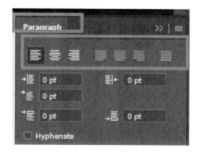

✦ Once you've chosen Justify, simply click ☑ in the choices menu to complete the process.

To rotate text(s)

✦ The text in the Photoshop document that you want to alter should be opened. Make sure the text you want to edit is on a type layer to enable editing.

✦ A type layer contains the text you wish to transfer; pick that layer.

✦ Select the **Move tool** from the **toolbar**.

- Click the text you want to transfer, then check **Auto Select Layer** and **Show Transform Controls** from the **Options bar**.
- Select the text by clicking it. The transform box surrounding your text will then be visible.
- Hover close to the transform box's corners. The cursor transforms into a double-headed arrow.
- To rotate the text in the desired direction, click and drag the curved arrow. In order to obtain a more precise rotation, you can also enter values in the options bar.
- You're finished after you click ✔ in the options bar!

CHAPTER EIGHT

TRANSFORMING IMAGES IN PHOTOSHOP

Introduction to the Transform Tool in Photoshop

One element of Photoshop that helps a user operate more efficiently is the transform tools. In Photoshop software, the transform tool allows us to scale up, rotate, flip, and do other types of transformations on the selected image. This chapter will go over how to use the transform tool in this program as well as how to manage the many parameters of this Photoshop function. So let's begin talking about this subject. The Keyboard shortcut for transforming tools in Photoshop is **Ctrl/Cmd + T**. After accessing the transform feature you can either left-click your mouse to open other transform options or you hold the Ctrl/Cmd key, Alt/Opt key or the Shift key individually or you hold them at once to access other transform options.

There are two major kinds of Transform tools in Photoshop; **Transform** and **Free Transform**. Numerous things we make are not always the perfect size, rotation, or skew that we desire. Using the Transform and Free Transform Tools, we may change or transform things.

Users can change their item or selection using the **Transform** feature in a number of different ways, including scaling, rotating, distorting, and flipping (mirror) while the **Free Transform** feature allows you to make several transformations at once, rather than one at a time.

What you will learn in this chapter.

- How to transform images, texts, shapes and other elements of design in Photoshop.
- How to use the Transform tool.
- How to use the Content-Aware tool.
- How to use the AI Generative fill.
- How to use the Content-Aware scale.
- How to use the crop tool and the other tools it houses.

Other transform Options in Photoshop

In Photoshop, the Free Transform and Transform gives you access to other transform options. The only difference between these two programs is just in how they carry out their operations. In this section, we will be examining the other transform options that are available in the Transform tool in Photoshop.

Scale
Rotate
Skew
Distort
Perspective

Warp
Split Warp Horizontally
Split Warp Vertically
Split Warp Crosswise
Remove Warp Split

Convert warp anchor point

Toggle Guides

Rotate 180°
Rotate 90° Clockwise
Rotate 90° Counter Clockwise

Flip Horizontal
Flip Vertical

✦ **Scale**: Scaling images is Free Transform's default action. Thus, whichever handle you move will scale the image. Hold the **Shift key** to scale your objects proportionally in Photoshop 2023. With Scaling you can increase or reduce the size of an object. Hold the **Alt/Opt key** to scale an image proportionally from the center.

✦ **Rotate**: This Transform option allows you to move your objects in a clockwise or anti-clockwise direction. You can access this feature by either going through the Transform options or you move your mouse cursor outside the Free Transform box where the cursor will change into a curved, double-sided arrow for rotation.

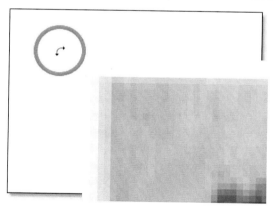

Use the Shift Key to constrain the rotation to 15-degree increments.

✦ **Skew**: Simply put, skewing occurs when an image is not straight. By holding down the Option (Alt) Key, Skew enables you to move a corner point independently or simultaneously with the one on the other side. Click on the top or bottom handle and drag to skew the image left or right with Skew selected:

✦ **Distort**: It's impressive how precisely you can deform objects to fit into specified places, so this is a wonderful alternative if an artist wants to replace a painting on a wall or change the wallpaper in a room. With distortion, you can pick up corner points for precise individual movement or center side points to manipulate the edge as desired.

✦ **Perspective**: Perspective conforms the distortion of an object to create a mathematical perspective. The item is warped from side to side if the center edge point is shifted.

If a corner point is adjusted, depending on whether you are expanding or reducing the Transform Box, both corners move inward or outward.

✦ **Warp:** When the Warp icon is clicked, a grid that can be manipulated at will to create unique distortions inside the Transforming command is displayed.

When making panoramas, this option can be very useful if the edges don't quite line up well.

Other transform options are:

✦ Rotate 180°
✦ Rotate 90° Clockwise
✦ Rotate 90° Counter Clockwise
✦ Flip Horizontal
✦ Flip Vertical

These options above are self-explanatory and widely used in picture editing to make rapid shape modifications.

Free Transform

The Free Transform command enables you to do many transformations (including rotation, scale, skew, distort, and perspective) at once. A warp transformation is another option. To transition between transformation kinds, you simply hold down a key on your keyboard rather than selecting various commands.

Follow the procedures below to use the Free Transform effectively,

✦ Select the object you want to transform
✦ Do one of the following to carry out the transform operation;
   o Select the **Free Transform** under **Edit** in the **Menu Bar** (upper-side of the Photoshop's workspace)

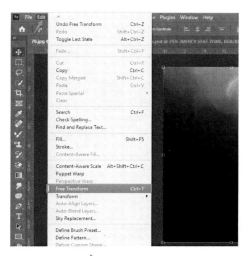

o Select the **Move tool** (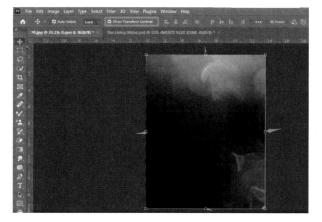)to change a selection, pixel-based layer, or **selection boundary**. Then, in the settings menu, choose **Show Transform Controls.**

o Choose the **Path Selection tool** (▶) to transform a vector shape or path. Then, in the settings menu, choose **Show Transform Controls.**

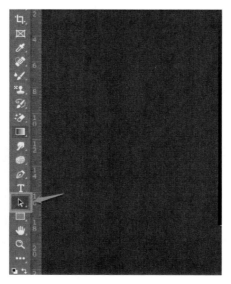

✦ Do one or more of the following:
  ○ To scale by dragging, do one of the following:
    ▪ Drag a corner handle to proportionately scale the layer if the Maintain Aspect Ratio button (Link icon) is selected in the Options

    bar.
    ▪ Drag a corner handle to scale the layer irregularly if the Options bar's Maintain Aspect Ratio button (Link icon) is deactivated.

    ▪ When transforming, keep holding down the Shift key to switch between proportional and non-proportional scaling behavior.
  ○ Enter percentages in the Width and Height text boxes in the options bar to scale numerically. To keep the aspect ratio, click the Link button.

  ○ Move the cursor outside the bounding border so that it forms a curved, two-sided arrow, and then drag to **rotate**. To limit the rotation to 15° increments, press **Shift**.

- Enter degrees in the rotation text box in the options bar to rotate numerically. △ 0.00 °
- Holding down the Alt or Option key while dragging a handle will cause the **distortion** to be relative to the center point of the enclosing border.
- Press Ctrl (Windows) or Command (Mac OS) and drag a handle to freely **distort**.
- Press Ctrl+Shift on a Windows or Mac computer to **skew**, then drag a side handle. The pointer transforms into a white arrowhead with a tiny double arrow when it is placed over a side handle.
- Enter degrees in the H (horizontal skew) and V (vertical skew) text boxes in H: 0.00 V: 0.00 the options bar to **skew** numerically.
- Press Ctrl+Alt+Shift (Windows) or Command+Option+Shift (Mac OS) and drag a corner handle to apply perspective. The pointer changes to a gray arrowhead when placed over a corner handle.
- Click the ☷ button labeled Switch Between Free Transform and Warp Modes in the settings box to warp. To change an item's shape, drag control points, or select a warp style from the Warp pop-up menu in the options bar. The shape of the warp can be modified with the square handle after selecting it from the Warp pop-up menu. ☷
- Click a square on the reference point locator in the options bar to change the reference point. ▦
- The X (horizontal position) and Y (vertical position) text boxes in the options bar must have values for the new location of the reference in order to move an item. To set the new position in relation to the present position, click the Relative Positioning button.

X: 1049.00 p △ Y: 1045.50 p

✦ After you done with your transformation and ready to save your transformation changes, click the Commit button✓ in the options bar, hit Return on a Mac or Windows computer, or double-click anywhere inside the transformation marquee.

⊘ ✓

✦ Press Esc or click the Cancel button in the options bar to stop the transformation.

196

Transform

Users can change their item or selection using the Transform feature in a number of different ways, including scaling, rotating, distorting, and flipping (mirror).

- ↕ Select a layer or make a new selection to use the transform function.
- ↕ Select **Transform** from the **Edit menu**, then choose the type of transformation you want to apply.

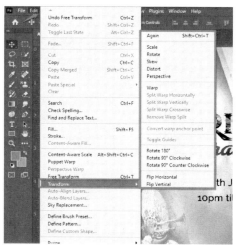

- ↕ Your selection will be surrounded by a bounding box that you can manipulate using the handles. Your image will automatically change if you choose Rotate 180°, Rotate 90°, Flip Horizontal, or Flip Vertical.

Content-Aware: Generative Fill, Content-Aware Fill, and Content-Aware Scale

These features in Photoshop are related to one another, one more advanced than the other. They are also used to solve different problems. They all use the Color algorithm to carry out their operation but their means of operation are not the same. In this section we will be studying the **AI Generative Fill**, **Content-Aware Fill** and the **Content-Aware Scale**. Other content-aware tools like the Content-Aware Move tool will be touched in the next chapter of retouching tools.

Using AI Generative Fill

Like every new update to Photoshop, this new feature is one of them. Unlike the other content-aware tools, using straightforward text prompts driven by Adobe Firefly generative AI, you can add and remove contents from using Adobe Photoshop's Generative Fill feature. The Generative Fill is made available by the contextual bar. There are three main uses of Generative Fill:

- ✦ To and remove replace objects in images.
- ✦ For Generative Fill Outcrop.
- ✦ For Generative Expand.

If you can`t seem to find your contextual task bar, do the following to enable it.

- ✦ Select **Window** from the **Menu Bar**.

- ✦ Scroll down and select **Contextual Taskbar** to enable it.

To effectively perform texts to image with the generative fill, do the following.

- ✦ Select the portion you want to remove and replace with any of the selection tools.

- Select **Generative Fill** on the **Contextual Taskbar,** and type in the description you desire and the selected area has itself automatically filled with it (Be sure to have an internet connection).
Options for your generated images will be made available in the **Properties Panel**.

To perform a generative fit outcrop, do the following.

- Open the image on Photoshop and select the **Crop Tool** from the **Menu Bar**.

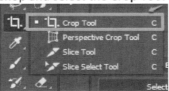

- Expand the Canvas around the image beyond the size of the image.

- Select **Generative Expand** on the contextual taskbar and click on **Generate** and the empty canvas will automatically fill itself up.

To perform a generative expand, do the following.

- Open the image on Photoshop and select the **Crop Tool** from the **Menu Bar**.

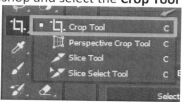

- Make your expansion with the **Crop tool**.

- Select **Generative Expand** in the **Option Settings**.

✦ Then, select **Generate** in the contextual taskbar.

Content-Aware Fill

With the help of the new Content-Aware function in Photoshop, you may edit photographs in a subtle manner. When you use Photoshop's Content Aware tool, it examines the nearby pixels and makes an educated guess as to what the missing pixels should be. This makes removing items from images without leaving a trace simple.

To use the content-aware fill, follow the instructions below;

✦ Simply use the lasso tool to pick the item you wish to remove.

✦ After creating your selection, use either of the following methods
  o Go to **Edit** > **Fill**

○ Left-click your mouse and a window pops up, Select **the Content-Aware Fill** for direct result or Select **Fill.**

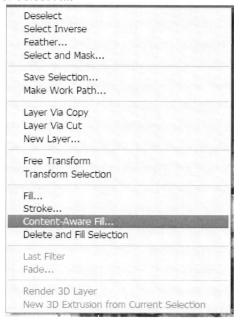

✦ After selecting **Fill**, A window pops up, From the **Contents** drop-down menu, select **Content-Aware.**

✦ Click **Ok** after you are done adjusting your settings (making adjustments to the settings are not always necessary)

✦ Now, leave the Content-Aware to perform its magic.

Content-Aware Scale

We may modify the size of an image without affecting the key components of the scene thanks to the content-aware scaling tool.

Resizing an image using the Content-Aware Scale preserves its essential visual elements, such as people, objects, animals, and so on. When resizing an image, content-aware scaling mostly affects pixels in regions without significant visual information, as opposed to standard scaling, which uniformly affects all pixels. You can upscale or downscale photos using Content-Aware Scale to enhance composition, fit a layout, or adjust the orientation. There is an option to set a ratio of content-aware scaling to standard scaling if you want to apply some normal scaling while resizing your image.

When resizing an image, Content-Aware Scale gives you the option to employ an alpha channel to protect specified sections of the image.

On layers and selections, content-aware scaling operates. Images can be in all bit depths and color modes, including RGB, CMYK, Lab, and Grayscale. Adjustment layers, layer masks, individual channels, Smart Objects, 3D layers, Video layers, several layers running at once, or layer groups are not compatible with content-aware scaling.

Follow the procedure below to use the content-aware scale effectively;

✦ Select the image you desire to scale
✦ From the **Edit Menu** in the **Menu bar**, Select **Content-Aware Scale**

- Choose one of the options listed below in the options bar:
  - ○ **Location of Reference Point**: To choose the fixed point that the image will be resized around, click a square (▦) on the reference point finder. By default, the image's focal point is in the middle.
  - ○ **Use a Reference Point in Relative Positioning:** To specify the reference point's new location in relation to its existing location, click the button.
  - ○ **Point of Reference Position**: This option places the reference point in that precise spot. Enter the pixel dimensions for the X- and Y-axes.
  - ○ **Scaling percentage**: provides an estimate of the image scaling in terms of the original size. Put a percentage in for the height (H) and width (W) (H). Click Maintain Aspect Ratio (⬚) if desired.
  - ○ **Amount**: specifies the proportion of content aware to standard scaling. By typing in the text box or clicking the arrow and dragging the slider, you can enter a percentage for content-aware scaling.
  - ○ **Protect**: Select an alpha channel that designates the protected area.
  - ○ **Protect skin tones**: This option tries to protect areas that have skin tones.

- To scale the image, drag a handle on the bounding box. Drag a corner handle while holding down Shift to scale accordingly. The pointer turns into a double arrow when it is over a handle.
- Either select Commit Transform (◎) or Cancel Transform (✔).

How to protect an object while using the content-aware scale

- ✦ Make a selection around the content you want to be protected, and then navigate to the **Select Menu** and select **Save Selection**.
- ✦ After saving your selection, you can then proceed to scaling the entire image.
- ✦ Select **Content-Aware Scale** under **Edit**.
- ✦ Select the produced alpha channel from the options bar.

- ✦ To scale the image, move a handle along the bounding border.

The Crop Tool and its other related tools

Apart from being a tool, the crop Tool also houses three other tools. They are The **Perspective Crop Tool**, **Slice Tool**, and The **Slice Select Tool.** In this section, we will be considering each of these tools.

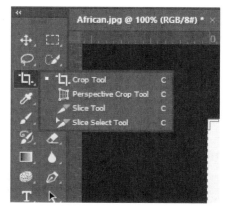

The Crop Tool

Cropping is the removal of some elements from a photo in order to sharpen the focus or improve the composition. In Photoshop, crop and straighten images with the Crop tool. The crop tool is non-destructive, and you have the option to keep the pixels you've cropped in order to refine the crop limits in the future. While cropping, the Crop tool offers simple ways to straighten a picture.

The Crop tool (⬚) allows you to select an area of an image and discard everything outside this area. The tool may be found on the left side of the Photoshop Toolbox, third from the top.

While cropping does result in a reduction in an image's size, it is not the same as scaling. Cropping does not change the size of the image's content at all, unlike resizing, which shrinks or enlarges the entire image and everything in it.

Follow the procedures below to use the crop tool effectively.

- Open your image in Photoshop
- Choose the Crop Tool from the toolbar. The photo's edges reveal crop borders.
- To define the crop limits of your image, either draw a new cropping region or move the corner and edge handles.
- If necessary, adjust the crop settings in the **Option bar**

- o **Size and Proportion**: Decide on a crop box ratio or size. Additionally, you have the option of selecting, entering, or even creating your own preset values for subsequent usage.

- o **Overlay Options**: Select a view to see cropping overlay guides in. There are other guides, including the Grid, Rule of Thirds, and Golden Ratio. Press O to go through every selection.

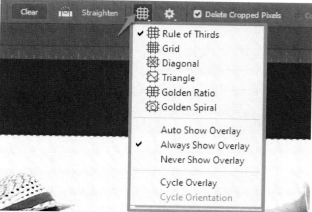

o **Crop Options**: You can specify additional crop choices by selecting the settings (tool) menu.

- **Use Classic mode**: If you want to use the Crop tool as it was in older versions of Photoshop, turn on this setting (CS5 and earlier).
- **Auto Center Preview**: To center the preview on the canvas, turn on this setting
- **Show Cropped Area**: To display the cropped area, turn on this option. Only the last area is previewed when this option is deactivated.
- **Enable Crop Shield**: To add a hue to the sections that were cropped, use the crop shield. You can choose an opacity and color. When you alter the crop boundaries, the opacity is increased if you enable auto adjust opacity

o **Delete Cropped Pixels**: To apply a non-destructive crop and keep pixels outside the crop limits, disable this option. No pixels are lost during non-destructive cropping. To view areas outside the current crop borders, click the image afterwards.

To eliminate any pixels that are outside the crop region, turn on this setting. These pixels are lost and cannot be recovered for alterations in the future.

o **Content-Aware**: When you use the Crop tool to resize your canvas, rotate a picture, or straighten it, Photoshop now uses content-aware technology to intelligently fill in the blanks.

✦ To crop the image, press Enter on a Windows computer or Return on a Mac.

Perspective Crop Tool

The perspective crop tool is the second tool nested in the crop tool. The perspective crop tool allows you to transform the perspective in an image while working. You may crop an image while changing the viewpoint using the Perspective Crop tool. When working with keystone-distorted photos, use the perspective crop tool. When an object is photographed at an angle as opposed to a straight-on view, keystone distortion happens. For instance, if you photograph a tall building from the ground up, the building's edges appear to be closer to one another at the top than they do at the bottom.

Follow the procedure below to use the perspective crop tool effectively.

✦ Open the image you desire to crop in Photoshop
✦ Select the image in the layer panel
✦ Select the **Perspective Crop Tool** from the **Crop Tool** in the **Toolbar**

✦ Draw a marquee around the misaligned object. Compare the marquee's edges to the object's rectangular edges.

♦ To finish the perspective crop, hit Enter (Windows) or Return (Mac OS).

The Slice Tool

The Slice Tool cuts a whole photoshop document into many slices as desired. The entire Photoshop document is divided into several slices using the slice tool. It enables users to divide a large image or piece of artwork into smaller pieces that fit together like jigsaw puzzles (but they all have straight edges). Alternatively, the slice tool aids in extracting a portion of the image without actually cutting or cropping it. When a single, large image needs to be divided into numerous smaller ones, it can be employed in a variety of situations. The image or diagram can be divided into square or rectangular portions.

The crop tool portion of the tool menu in Photoshop includes a slice tool.

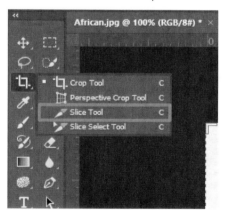

To use the Slice tool effectively, follow the procedures below.

♦ Launch your image in Photoshop
♦ Select the **Slice Tool** from the **Crop Tool** nest in the **Toolbar**.
♦ Adjust the settings of the tool in the **Options bar** (if Necessary)

- ○ **Style**: Three options exist for style: Normal, Fixed Aspect Ratio, and Fixed Size.

  - ▪ **Normal**: This choice is already chosen. It produces regular slices of any size and aspect ratio.
  - ▪ **Fixed aspect** ratio: The choices under this option are made in accordance with a fixed aspect ratio (i.e width to height ratio). The width and height values are movable. Assume that the dimensions are 2 and 3. It will always produce slices with a width:height ratio of 2:3.
  - ▪ **Fixed Size**: With this choice, we can specify the slice's height and breadth in pixels.
- ○ **Height & Width**: When the style option is fixed aspect ratio or fixed size, these options are used to set the height and width of the selection.
- ○ **Slice from Guides**: With the aid of the rulers' guidance, we can also cut slices.

❖ Now cut a piece of the image from the desired location. You will observe that once the first slice is drawn, Photoshop automatically creates further slices to match the rest of the document.

❖ After making your slices, Go to the **File menu** after making and choose the option to **save for the web** in the **Export** Section.

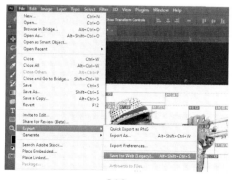

✦ A dialogue box appears on the screen, use the Shift key to select each of the slices that you have created.

✦ Go to the **Preset Option** and select the format that you want to save your slices in.

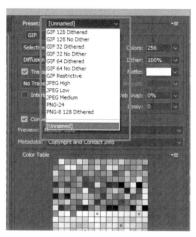

✦ A dialog box with the option to preserve the default settings comes on the screen after you click the **Save** button. In the dialog box, select **Save** to finally save your work.

The Select Slice Tool

The primary operation of the Slice Select Tool is to assist in selecting a certain slice. It is a very practical and effective application for managing slices and features a variety of functionality, including the ability to move slices, scale them, and arrange them on slides. In the settings menu, the slice select tool is located underneath the slice tool.

Follow the procedure below to use the Select Slice Tool effectively.

✦ Open your image in Photoshop

✦ After creating slices from your image, you need the Select Slice Tool to select each slice. So select the **Select slice tool** from the **Crop Tool** nest in the **Toolbar**.

211

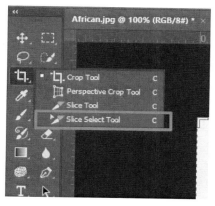

- The size of the slice can now be adjusted, and it can also be moved. Holding the SHIFT key while using the slice choose tool will allow you to move the slice in a straight line both horizontally and vertically.
- Adjust the tool's settings on the **Option Bar**, if necessary.

- Ordering: There are four ways to order a certain slice, and they are as follows:

  Starting from the left, we have:

  - **Bring to front**: Using this choice, the slice is brought to the front.
  - **Bring to forward**: This choice is used to incrementally bring the slice to the top. If there are two slices above the current slice, clicking this option once will move the slice to position two, and clicking it again will move it to the top (i.e number one).
  - **Bring downward**: In the same manner as the preceding choice, but in the reverse order, this option is used to bring the slice to the bottom in steps.
  - **Bring to bottom**: By selecting this option, the slice is brought to the bottom.
- Promote: With this option, an automatic slice is changed into a user-defined slice. Now, the question of how to tell if it is an auto slice or user slice can

212

come up. The answer is that while a human slice can be adjusted using the slice choose tool, auto slices do not have a scaling option activated within them.

o **Divide**: By choosing this option, the user can divide the chosen slice into a number of smaller slices.

A dialog box similar to the one below will appear when you select the Divide option:

As you can see, the dialog box is divided into two parts:

- **Horizontal Slice**: When selected, this option creates horizontal slices out of the slice.
- **Vertical Slice**: When selected, this option creates vertical slices out of the slice.

The following choices are now available in both sections:

- **Slices down, evenly spaced**: The user-specified number of evenly spaced slices is what this option does.
- **Pixels per slice**: The user-specified number of pixels is used to determine how many slices are made.

o **Align**: For two or more chosen slices, there are numerous alignment choices. Now, the topic of how to choose several slices can come up. The SHIFT key must be held down in order to choose numerous levels while using the slice select tool.

Below are the alternatives that are aligned:

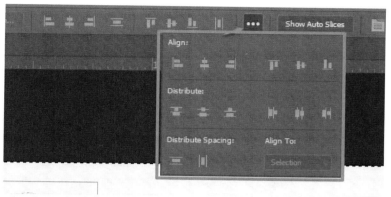

Starting from the left,

- **Align left edges**: The left edges of the chosen slice are aligned using this option.
- **Align center:** This choice is used to center the slices.
- **Align right edges**: Using this option, the right edges of the chosen slice are aligned.
- **Vertically Distribute**: This option is used to vertically distribute the layers that have been chosen.
- **Align top edges**: Using this option, the top edges of the chosen slices are aligned.
- **Align to slice center**: Using this option, you can align to the slice centers you've chosen.
- **Align the bottom edges**: The bottom edges of the chosen slices are aligned using this option.
- **Distribute horizontally**: Using this option, the chosen layers are distributed horizontally.

○ **Show/Hide Auto Slice**: Since we already know this, whenever we use the Slice tool to make a slice, Photoshop also creates slices for the rest of the document. So, we can display or conceal the auto slices Photoshop generates using the Show/Hide Auto Slice option.

CHAPTER NINE

RETOUCHING TOOLS IN PHOTOSHOP

Image Retouching in Photoshop

This aspect of Photoshop is essential to social media design and photography. When speaking about photography, terms like "airbrushing," "post-production," "photo retouching," and "photo editing" are frequently misinterpreted. Some photographers use these terms to signify different things, even though they are all related to image manipulation. We've decided to go a little further and explain the variations between these expressions to give you a better idea of what outcomes you can expect from your photography or photo retouching service.

Photo Retouching

The process of eliminating any imperfections from an image is referred to as "photo retouching". This usually involves adjusting the color and tone, eliminating dark circles under the eyes, and adjusting the brightness, contrast, and saturation. In addition, airbrushing—the process of either adding or removing background elements from the image—may also be a part of picture retouching on occasion.

Photo Editing

Cropping, adjusting exposure, and adjusting color temperature are all part of photo editing. It should be noted that the terms "photo retouching" and "photo editing" are sometimes used synonymously. Furthermore, some photographers assert that editing comprises going through the raw files from the photo shoot and picking only the best images from the gallery.

What you will learn in this chapter.

- **The different terms used in Photo Editing.**
- **How to use all the retouching tools in Photoshop; Spot Healing Brush, Healing Brush, Patch Tool, Content-Aware Move Tool, Red Eye Tool, Clone Stamp Tool, Blur Tool, Sharpen Tool, Smudge Tool, Dodge Tool, Burn Tool, Sponge Tool, etc.**
- **The relationship between The History Panel and the History Brush Tool.**

Photo Enhancing

Photo enhancement usually means making the image look better overall. Toning, vignetting, and changing the color scheme (to black and white) are a few examples. After retouching, enhancement is carried out to guarantee that the colors are consistent throughout the gallery and to imbue each event photo with a distinct atmosphere.

Post-Production/ Post-Processing

Post Production/Post Processing basically refers to all of the previously discussed topics. It comprises modifying the photos in any way after they have been taken.

Please be advised that depending on the professional, each type of post-production service has a different meaning. Therefore, you would need to speak with your photography or photo-retouching company to find out exactly what adjustments will be made to your images.

NOTE: All the concepts defined above are mostly used in the photography niche.

Retouching Tools in Photoshop

Among the several tools offered by Photoshop. Professionals employ Photoshop's primary photo-retouching tools to provide amazing finishing touches to photographs. The usage of these tools, which you can find in Photoshop's tools panel, makes retouching photographs easier. The retouching tools in Photoshop are **Healing Brush Tool**, **Spot Healing Tool**, **Red Eye**, **Patch Tool**, **Content-Aware Tool**, **Clone Stamp Tool**, **Dodge, Sponge, and Burn Tool**, **Blur and Sharpen Tool**, **The Color Replacement Tool**, **Pattern Stamp Tool**.

The Spot Healing Brush

The Spot Healing Brush is nested with other retouching tools in the Tools Menu in Photoshop and they are The Healing Brush Tool, Patch tool, Content-Aware Move Tool and Red Eye Tool.

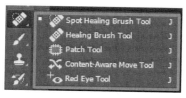

The Spot Healing Brush corrects minor imperfections and blemishes, as well as dust spots. It is used to remove unwanted spots or small objects from images. The smaller the object you remove, the better the likelihood that the Spot Healing Brush does it in a seamless way. Removing objects from your photo also works better on areas with less detail, like the sky or the water.

Follow the instructions below to use this tool.

- After opening your image, create a new layer by clicking on the plus icon below the layer panel. Why do this? It ensures that your original image is not altered and your modifications are non-destructible.

- Once you have created a blank layer, select the spot healing brush from the tool menu or press **J** on your keyboard to instantly access the spot healing brush.

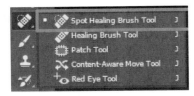

- After selecting your spot healing brush, adjust its settings in the **Options Bar.** How do I do this?
  - Be sure that **Sample All layers** is checked.
  - The mode should be set to **Normal** and the type to **Content-Aware**

  - The **Brush Angle** does not matter as long as you are using a perfectly round brush.

- Adjust your brush settings in the brush panel adjacent to **Mode.**

- o Depending on what you want to get rid of in your shot, you can change the size of the brush. The ideal size adjustment is to make yourself just big enough to cover the flaw but not any bigger. For the majority of photos, having a hardness of 50% and a spacing of 25% works excellent. For a properly-rounded brush, make sure the roundness setting is 100%.
- ✦ Then you can start to retouch your image.

While we have only used one kind of Spot Healing Brush, there are a few other choices that you can explore:

- ✦ **Mode**: The Spot Healing Brush has several operating modes, including Normal, Multiply, Screen, Color, and Luminosity. These modes all do a few varying tasks. In essence, they instruct Photoshop on how to make the new pixels blend in with the old ones. You probably won't ever need to utilize any of these options to alter your photographs, though.
- ✦ **Type**: Content-Aware, Create Texture, and Proximity Match are the three options available in this option.
  - o **Content-Aware**: In most cases, Content Aware will be your best choice for spot healing. In this iteration of the Spot Healing Brush, Photoshop analyzes your image automatically to determine which pixels should be used in place of the ones you want to repair.
  - o **Create Texture**: Photoshop will construct a pattern of the pixels nearby the image you wish to replace when you use the Create Texture Spot Healing Brush. For textured patterns that need to precisely realign, this can work incredibly well.
  - o **Proximity Match**: In order to discover matching pixels to replace, Proximity Match looks at the pixels immediately surrounding the area you are repairing. When spot-healing a tiny region that perfectly matches the

218

surrounding areas, this variant of the Spot Healing Brush performs effectively.

- **Spacing**: You may modify how smooth the brush appears when you click and drag by using the spacing option. The majority of photos will work flawlessly at 25%. The brush will be as smooth as it can be at 0%. Even when you click and drag, the Spot Healing Brush will have spread out spots at a 1,000% spacing.
- **Angle/Roundness**: You can modify the brush's shape using the angle and roundness options. The brush is a flawless circle when it is perfectly round. However, decreasing the roundness will alter the brush's shape, and changing the angle will alter how the oval is rotated. In some cases, spot removal can benefit from this. Most of the time, you won't need to utilize these options.

The Healing Brush

The Healing Brush tool is used to remove blemishes, imperfections, and irregular skin tones. It achieves this by fusing them with the pixels in the surrounding image. Similar to how the Clone Stamp tool functions, so does the Healing Brush Tool. The Healing Brush Tool, on the other hand, also replicates the texture, shading, and lighting of the source pixels in the sampled pixels. As a result, the copied pixels fit in perfectly with their new surroundings.

Follow the instructions below to use this tool

- After opening your image, duplicate your original image and ensure that every modification is done to the duplicated image. Why do this? It ensures that your original image is not altered and your modifications are non-destructive.
- From the toolbar, choose the Healing Brush tool ✐ (J). I if you can't find the Healing Brush tool, click and hold the Spot Healing Brush tool first. Then, choose the Healing Brush tool.

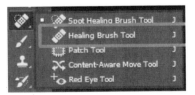

- Adjust its settings in the **Options Bar** if necessary by clicking the brush sample in the tool options bar to bring up a pop-up window where you can select the **Brush Size**, **Mode**, **Source**, **Aligned**, **Sample**, and **Diffusion** parameters.

- Ensure that **Sampled** is checked in your **Source option,** Your **Mode** is **Normal** and your **Sample** is in **Current Layer.**

- Position the pointer over a region in your image and Alt-click (Windows) or Option-click to set the source sampling area (Mac).
- After sampling the region of your choice as stated in the previous instruction, move your brush over the area you want to retouch. Each time you let go of the mouse button, the sampled pixels are combined with the already-existing pixels.

The Healing Brush Option Settings

You can use the Healing Brush tool's various parameters to increase your success in resolving particular problems. The Options Bar displays the healing brush settings once it is selected.

- **Brush**: You must select a brush in Photoshop before you can paint with any tool. To choose the tool's brush size, shape, and hardness, click the brush option.

- ○ **Size**: The size of the brush is the first consideration while picking one for healing. In general, pick a brush that is roughly twice as large as the blemish at its broadest point. The majority of scratches are rather tiny; if you make the brush too large, it will be difficult to prevent the sample area from straying over pixels that don't correspond to the area you're trying to correct.
- ○ **Hardness**: To adjust a brush's hardness, take the following actions:
  The Brush button is located on the Options bar.
  Set the hardness slider to a value lower than 100% by dragging it to the left.

- **Mode**: The Normal, Replace, Multiply, Screen, Darken, Color, and Luminosity operating modes are just a few of the options available for the Healing Brush. These modes each perform a few different functions. In essence, they give Photoshop instructions on how to blend in the new pixels with the old ones. Most likely, you won't ever need to use any of these tools to edit your photos.

- **Source**: This determines the source from which you want to pick your sampling region for retouching. There are two options available in the source feature.

  o **Sampled:** allows you to pick any region of your image as a sampling source for heal.
  o **Pattern:** allows you to pick the preset patterns in your Photoshop as a sampling source for heal.
- **Aligned**: The Aligned gadget on the Options bar forces the starting point to follow your cursor even after you have finished a stroke. In contrast to leaving it off, which causes the sample point to start at its original location at the beginning of each stroke.
- **Use Legacy**: allows you to use the algorithm of the legacy healing brush available in Photoshop CC 2014
- **Sample**: allows you to decide the range of layers you want your healing effects to apply either **Current layer, Current & Below, or All layers**

- **Diffusion:** When utilizing the healing brush, there is a setting named "diffusion" in the Option Bar. From a drop-down menu, select a number between 1 and 7. How many pixels are spread out around your brush depends on that quantity. The least amount of dispersion occurs when the diffusion is set to 1.

The Patch Tool

You can edit your images with the Patch Tool, which is a feature of Adobe Photoshop. It belongs to the Spot Healing Brush group since their functions are comparable. However, this tool operates by picking a portion of the image, as opposed to the Spot Healing Brush, which operates by brushing on the image.

In a word, the Patch Tool has two functions: duplicating and removing elements.

As stated earlier, The Patch Tool is used for duplicating/cloning elements or to completely remove them.

To **remove unwanted elements** with the patch tool, follow the procedure below,

- Open the image you want to retouch. You may as well duplicate your image and ensure that every modification is done on the duplicated image to prevent damaging the original image and the duplicated serves as a safe and new canvas for experiment.
- Select the **Patch Tool** from the **Tool Menu** in **The Spot Healing Brush Nest**

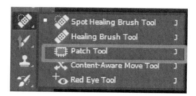

- Adjust the tool`s settings in the **Option bar** if necessary.

- Ensure that **Source** is checked and **Destination** is left unchecked in the **Options Bar**. **Source** allows you to remove an element completely while **Destinations** clones a selected object.

- Create a selection around the element you want to remove from the image
- Drag you selection to the part you want to replace it with. In reality, the area you selected after dragging the initial selection overrides the area you initially selected.

To clone an element with the patch tool, follow the procedure below,

✢ Open the image you want to retouch. You may as well duplicate your image and ensure that every modification is done on the duplicated image to prevent damaging the original image and the duplicated serves as a safe and new canvas for experiment.

✢ Select the **Patch Tool** from the **Tool Menu** in **The Spot Healing Brush Nest**

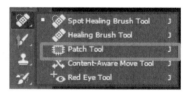

✢ Adjust the tool`s settings in the **Option bar** if necessary.

✢ Ensure that **Destination** is checked while **Source** is left unchecked in the **Options Bar**. **Source** allows you to remove an element completely while **Destinations** clones a selected object.

✢ Create a selection around the image you want to clone.
✢ Drag your selection to any desired region in the image to duplicate it there

The Patch Tool Option Settings

- **The Selection Types**: These options determine how your selections interacts with each other. They are located at the upper-left of the **Option Bar.**

   ○ A Square ▣ (New Selection) allows you to draw a new selection
   ○ The Overlapping Squares ▣ (Add to Selection) allows you to add to previous selections
   ○ A filled and an empty square ▣ (Subtract from selection): allows you to remove the new selection from the previous one. Another way to use this

feature is to hold the Alt Key (Windows) or Option Key (macOS) while making a new selection.

- o The Second Overlapping Square  (Overlap Selection): allows you to keep the area shared by the new and previous selections.

✥ **The Content-Aware Patch**: The Patch Tool has two settings: **Content-Aware** and **Normal**. We utilized the Normal mode on the previous section. When we select Content-Aware, the patch will synthesize neighboring content for seamless blending with the surrounding content, which is the difference between Normal and Content-Aware.

On the Content-Aware option bar, there are several options to adjust.

- o **Structure**: Changing the degree to which the patch should replicate current image patterns. The patch adheres strongly to pre-existing image patterns when you set it to maximum (7). The patch only conforms roughly to pre-existing visual patterns when you set it to minimal (1).
- o **Color**: modifying the patch's color blending's intensity. Color mixing is disabled if you enter 0. Maximum color blending will be applied if you enter 10.
- o **Sample All Layers**: To generate the move in a different layer utilizing data from all layers, enable this option. In the Layers panel, select the desired layer.

✥ **Source & Destination**: **Source** allows you to remove an element completely while **Destination** clones a selected object.
✥ **Transparency**: When enabled, this option blends the patched part using a transparency factor.
✥ **Pattern**: This choice enables you to patch the area of the image that with the presets patterns in your Photoshop.
✥ **Diffusion**: This selection indicates how quickly the patched area catches up to the pixels around it. The better the diffusion, the higher the value. It has a range of 1 to 7 and is set to 5 by default.

Content-Aware Move Tool

Using the Content Aware Move tool, you may pick an element to move from one photo to another while smoothly positioning it so that it appears to belong there. You can

accomplish this without having to have expert-level Photoshop skills thanks to th
program.

Cutting and pasting an image from one photo into another is quite simple, but making th
alteration look natural and seamless so that it doesn't look "Photoshopped" is
completely different matter. The Content Aware Move tool can be used in this situatior

This tool may be found directly beneath your Patch Tool and Spot Healing Brush Tool.

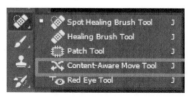

In a word, the Content-Aware Tool has two functions: Moving and duplicating elements

Follow the procedures below to **move** an object in Photoshop seamlessly with th
content-aware tool,

- ❖ Start by opening the photo you want to edit. You might as well make a copy of you
  image and make sure that all changes are made to the copy rather than the origin.
  in order to protect the original and use the copy as a secure and fresh canvas fo
  experimentation.
- ❖ Select the **Content-Aware Tool** in the **Tool Menu** from the Spot Healing Brus
  Nest.

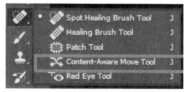

- ❖ Adjust its settings in the **Options Bar** and let the **Mode** be set on **Move, Transfor**
  On Drop should be checked too

- ❖ Create a selection around the object you desire to move
- ❖ Drag the object to the place of your choice and transform it to the size of you
  choice.

Follow the procedure below to duplicate an object seamlessly with the content-aware tool in Photoshop,

- As usual, start by opening the photo you want to edit. You might as well make a copy of your image and make sure that all changes are made to the copy rather than the original in order to protect the original and use the copy as a secure and fresh canvas for experimentation
- Select the **Content-Aware Tool** in the **Tool Menu** from the Spot Healing Brush Nest.

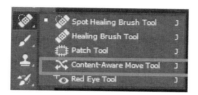

- Adjust its settings in the **Options Bar** and let the **Mode** be set on **Extend**, **Transform On Drop** should be checked too.

- Create a selection around the object you desire to duplicate.
- Drag your selection to the place of your choice and transform it to the size of your choice.

The Content-Aware Tool Option Settings

- **Selection Types**: The selection properties apply to this property as well. There are four selection attributes, and Normal mode is the default setting.

- o **Normal** ▣: This is the selection you make with the content aware tool on a regular basis.
- o More pieces can be added to your patch selection using the **Add to Selection(**▣**)** selection feature than we can with the content-aware tool.
- o **Remove selection (**▣**)**: Using this selection attribute, you can opt to take out some of the already-selected pieces that need to be repaired.

- o **Intersect Selections** (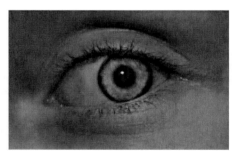)Selections that are common to two other selections are taken into account by this attribute, which functions similarly to an intersection.
- ✜ **Mode**: This option allows you to explore the two distinct functions of the content-aware tool.
  - o **Move:** This feature allows you to completely move elements in Photoshop
  - o **Extend:** This is a feature in the content-aware tool that allows you to duplicate the elements of an image.
- ✜ **Structure**: This feature is used to the control the end result of your work. With Structure you can instruct the program to match the edit's structure as closely as possible to the original texture.
- ✜ **Color**: Like the structure, color is used to control the end result of your work. With the aid of color, you can choose how closely the color of the content you are relocating will resemble the color of the material it is replacing.
- ✜ **Sample All layers**: Like it is present in other retouching tools, it is used to generate the move in a different layer utilizing data from all layers, enable this option. In the Layers panel, select the desired layer.
- ✜ **Transform On Drop**: allows you to manipulate the size of the object before finalizing your work.

Red Eye Tool

Like the name implies, the red eye tool is used to remove the red color and change it to a natural black pupil color. The Red eye tool is used on an eye image that contains a red color.

The **Red Eye Tool** is located in the **Tool Menu** in the Spot Healing Brush Nest.

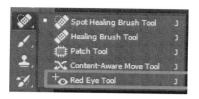

What causes Red Eye?

Low light photography results in the flash being activated very near the subject's face. The light is reflected off the subject's pupils. The light is reflecting off the blood vessels behind the eyes, making the pupils look bright red rather than their natural color of black. When you know what causes it, it's simple to correct, but it can give your subjects a demon-like appearance.

When an on-camera flash bounces off of the subject's eyes and shows in the image, red eye occurs, turning the subject's eye red.

How do I use the Red Eye Tool?

- Navigate to the toolbar on the left.
- "Spot Healing Brush Tool" should be selected.
- The "Red Eye Tool" is located at the bottom of the "Spot Healing Brush Tool" menu.

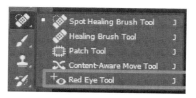

- Make sure Pupil Size and Darken Amount are both set to 50% in the top left-hand corner of the menu. (This is a best practice) Adjust the settings if you want to use a different approach.

- Finally, Make a selection round the red eye and then unclick, the red eye should be gone.

Clone Stamp Tool

The Clone stamp Tool is effective when you need to precisely duplicate color and detail from one section of an image to another. The Clone Stamp tool in Photoshop duplicates one portion of a picture onto another portion of the same image. The Clone Stamp tool is frequently used by photographers and designers to eliminate distracting aspects from a shot. For instance, it can be used to eliminate trees from a mountain vista by duplicating portions of the sky over them or to disguise deformities on people's faces by copying from another region of the skin.

In one word, The Clone Stamp is used for removing and duplicating elements in Photoshop.

Follow the instructions below to use effectively use the Clone Stamp Tool.

✤ Open up the image you want to retouch in Photoshop. You can either duplicate your original image and work on your new copy or add a new blank layer to your image.

✤ Navigate to the **Tool Menu** and select the **Clone Stamp Tool**.

✤ Adjust the tool`s settings at **Option Bar** to suit your desire. If you`re making your modifications to a duplicate copy of the original image, you can set your **sample** at **Current Layer/All layers** but if you`re working on a new blank layer, set your sample at **All layers/Current & Below.**

- Alt-click (Windows) or Option-click (MacOS) a region of detail to set the sample point (the sample point is your source region, that is, the area you are copying the duplicate you want to make from) when the Clone Stamp tool is active. The level of detail you'll need for retouching is displayed in a preview inside the Clone Stamp pointer. To align sampled detail with other areas of the image, use the preview.
- To cover an item, lightly brush over the region where you wish to add the sampled detail. A crosshair shows you where the detail is copied from as you work.
- Inspect the results to check for repeating details, you can use the clone stamp tool again to make minor adjustments.

The Clone Stamp Tool Option Settings

- **Brush**: You must select a brush in Photoshop before you can paint with any tool. To choose the tool's brush size, shape, and hardness, click the brush option.

- o **Size**: The size of the brush is the first consideration while picking one for Cloning
- o **Hardness**: To adjust a brush's hardness, take the following actions:
  The Brush button is located on the Options bar.
  Set the hardness slider to a value lower than 100% by dragging it to the left.
- **Mode**: The operating modes are just a few of the options available for the Clone Stamp Tool. These modes each perform a few different functions. In essence, they give Photoshop instructions on how to blend in the new pixels with the old ones. Most likely, you won't ever need to use any of these tools to edit your photos.

✦ **Opacity**: This feature specifies the level of transparency with which your brush will paint over the desired area. Adjust the Opacity slider to determine the level of opacity.

✦ **Aligned**: If you choose this option, drawing on the newly cloned image will continue even if you let go of the mouse button in the middle of it. When you remove the mouse button and pick up painting again when it is deselected, the clone will start drawing at the sampling point.

✦ **Sample**: determines the layer(s) your cloning will have visible effects on.

✦ **Flow**: indicates the intensity of the brush you are cloning with. You adjust the slider to make changes to your flow.

Pattern Stamp Brush

With the Pattern Stamp tool, you can paint a pattern or use a pattern from the pattern libraries to fill a selection or layer. You can choose from a variety of patterns in Photoshop

231

The Pattern Stamp Brush is nested in The Clone Stamp Tool. It paints a selected pattern over an image.

How do I use The Pattern Stamp Brush?

✥ Select the Pattern Stamp tool from the **Tool Menu**. (If you don't see it in the toolbox, click the Pattern Stamp tool icon in the Tool Options bar after choosing the Clone Stamp tool.)

✥ From the Pattern pop-up menu in the **Tool Options bar**, select a pattern. You can choose a library name from the panel menu to load it, or you can choose Load Patterns and go to the folder where the library is kept. Additionally, you can create your own pattern.

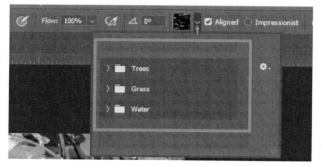

✥ Then brush your pattern on your image.

The Pattern Stamp Brush Settings

✥ **Brush**: Set the brush tip. After selecting a brush category from the Brush drop-down menu by clicking the arrow next to the brush sample, select a brush thumbnail.
✥ **Impressionist**: Use paint daubers to apply impressionist painting techniques to the pattern.

- ✦ **Size**: sets the brush's size in pixels. Enter a size in the text box or move the Size slider.
- ✦ **Opacity**: determines the transparency of the pattern you apply. When the opacity is set to a low value, pixels beneath a pattern stroke can be seen. Enter an opacity value or move the slider.
- ✦ **Mode**: Indicates how the paint you apply will interact with the picture's existing pixels. Blending modes are discussed there.
- ✦ Aligned: the pattern in a continuous, unified pattern. From one paintbrush stroke to the next, the pattern is in alignment. When you stop and start painting, the pattern will always be centered on the pointer if **Aligned** is deselected.

The Blur Tool, Sharpen Tool and Smudge Tool

These three tools are nested together in a tool group in Photoshop's Tool Menu. They are also called the **Focus Tools** These tools are used for retouching in Photoshop.

The uneven areas of an image can be softened or hardened with the "**Blur Tool**." To improve an image's contrast and clarity, utilize the "**Sharpen tool**." To combine the portions of an image, the "**Smudge tool**" is employed. Let's quickly explore each focal tool.

The Blur Tool

The blur tool blurs an image or is typically used to soften an image's sharp pixels. It can also give the image a creative touch, but how it does so will only be determined by how you use the tool.

The contrast between adjacent pixels is lessened when using the blur tool. The blur tool's icon resembles *a droplet of water that is about to fall* (.)

The **Options Bar** in the upper side of the workspace contains the settings of the blur tool like every other tool in Photoshop.

233

✤ **Brush**: This tool offers the same brush options as a brush tool or an eraser tool since it applies the effect using the brush tip. Before using any tool in Photoshop, you must first choose a brush. Click the brush option to select the brush's size, shape, and hardness.

- ○ Size: When choosing a brush for cloning, size is the first factor to take into account.
- ○ Hardness: The following steps should be taken to modify a brush's hardness: On the Options bar is where you'll find the Brush button.
  Drag the hardness slider to the left to drop the value below 100%.

✤ **Modes**: The Blur Tool has a number of different choices, including several working modes. Each of these modes carries out a variety of tasks. To put it simply, they advise Photoshop on how to mix in the new and old pixels. You most likely won't ever need to edit images using any of these programs.

✤ **Strength**: You can also modify the brush's strength to lessen the blur effect by adjusting the slider or input a specific figure in the slider's box.

- **Sample All Layers**: Having this effect checked allows your modifications to affect all layers, current, below and above.

How do I use The Blur Tool?

- Open up the image you want to retouch in Photoshop. You can either duplicate your original image and work on your new copy or add a new blank layer to your image. Ensure that **Sample All layers** is checked
- Select the Blur tool from the Tool Menu

- Adjust your brush settings in the **Options Bar** if necessary.

- Paint your brush over the area you want to modify.

The Sharpen Tool

The second item in the fly-out menu for the blur tool is the sharpen tool. Its icon resembles a pointed triangle ($\triangle$).

The sharpen tool improves the pixel contrast and brings more attention to the image. You must be very careful when using this tool because "sharpening" any part of the image will make that part stand out. So be careful not to over-sharpen it.

How do I use The Sharpen Tool?

- Like you did for other retouching tools, open up the image you want to retouch in Photoshop. You can either duplicate your original image and work on your new copy or add a new blank layer to your image. Ensure that **Sample All layers** is checked
- Select **The Sharpen Tool** from the **Tool Menu** under the **Blur`s tool drop-down tool options.**

✤ Adjust the tool's settings in the **Options Bar** to your desired taste. It is advisable to keep the value of the tool's strength under 25% to make subtle effects on your work.

✤ Paint your brush over the area you want to modify.

The Sharpen Tool's Options Setting

✤ **Brush**: This tool offers the same brush options as a brush tool or an eraser tool since it applies the effect using the brush tip. Before using any tool in Photoshop, you must first choose a brush. Click the brush option to select the brush's size, shape, and hardness.

236

- o Size: When choosing a brush for cloning, size is the first factor to take into account.
- o Hardness: The following steps should be taken to modify a brush's hardness: On the Options bar is where you'll find the Brush button.
  Drag the hardness slider to the left to drop the value below 100%.
- ❖ **Modes**: The Sharpen Tool has a number of different choices, including several working modes. Each of these modes carries out a variety of tasks. To put it simply, they advise Photoshop on how to mix in the new and old pixels. You most likely won't ever need to edit images using any of these programs.

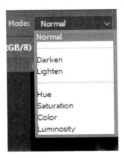

- ❖ **Strength**: You can also modify the brush's strength to lessen the sharpening effects by adjusting the slider or input a specific figure in the slider`s box.

- ❖ **Sample All Layers**: Having this effect checked allows your modifications to affect all layers, current, below and above. This option is very useful when you have multiple layers.

- ❖ **Protect Detail**: This option applies localized sharpening in a regulated way.

The Smudge Tool

This is the third and last tool in the blur tool's fly-out menu. As it is used to smooth an image, it is fairly similar to the blur tool. In the liquify option, this tool behaves almost like a warping effect.

The Smudge Tool mimics smudging paint with your finger and is designed to be used when painting. similar to how artists work while drawing traditionally. However, the tool can still be utilized to make spot edits.

The pixels are pushed around the canvas like wet paint that is being smudged. Thus, the moniker "smudge tool 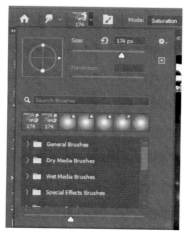." was born. If you want to give your image a creative, digitally painted effect, the smudge tool is really helpful.

You choose the layer you want to paint on when using the smudge tool. It blends all the pixels together from when you first started painting.

The Smudge Tool's Options Setting

- **Brush**: Pick any brush of your choice from the brush presets, and click the brush option to select the brush's size, shape, and hardness.
    - Size: When choosing a brush for cloning, size is the first factor to take into account. Unlike other retouching tools, The Smudge tool does not consider brush hardness.

- **Mode**: There are numerous options available for the Smudge Tool, including various operating modes. These modes each do different functions. Simply put, they offer Photoshop advice on how to blend in the new and old pixels. Most likely, none of these programs will ever be required for image editing.
- **Strength**: similar to the Sharpen and Blur Tools. The strength setting on the Smudge Tool controls how significantly your strokes will impact the image. More pixels will be moved by your strokes the stronger the strength.
- **Sample All Layers**: The sample all layers' option should be selected if your image contains more than one layer so that editing will only be done on the active layer.
- **Finger Painting**: The smudge tool adds a small stroke to the image when this option is checked, which is somewhat helpful if you want to utilize the tool for painting and color blending.

How do I use The Smudge Tool?

- Similar to the blur and sharpen tools, open up the image you want to retouch in Photoshop. You can either duplicate your original image and work on your new copy or add a new blank layer to your image. Ensure that **Sample All layers** is checked
- Select **The Smudge Tool** from the **Tool Menu** under the **Blur`s tool drop-down tool options.**

- Adjust the Tool`s setting in the **Options Bar** if necessary.

✦ Paint your brush over the area you want to modify.

The Dodge Tool, Burn Tool, and Sponge Tool

The Dodge, Burn, and Sponge tools in Adobe Photoshop are excellent for changing the focus point of a shot that didn't turn out as you had anticipated. They are based on traditional darkroom methods for fixing overexposed or underexposed areas of a photo.

You can access these tools in the Tools Menu on the left side of the Workspace,

The Shortcut command for accessing these tools is letter **O.** These triad tools are nested together.

Simply put, the Dodge tool lightens, the Burn tool darkens, and the Sponge tool saturates or desaturates the color in an area. There are a few things you should be aware of before using these controls and this controls also apply to other retouching tools like the Healing Brush, Spot Healing Brush, Clone Stamp Tool, Blur Tool, Sharpen Tool, Smudge Tool, etc.:

✦ Editing methods that cause destruction include Dodge, Burn, and Sponge. That implies that the adjustments are made directly to the picture. It's a good idea to avoid working on the background layer because of this. If you go too far, you can discard errors by creating duplicate layers and working with those.

✦ These items are brushes, so you can use them to "paint." By hitting the [and [keys, you can make the brush bigger or smaller, respectively.

Note the following about this Triad tools.

✦ **Highlights:** consists of the brightest areas and it permits modifications to these areas

- **Shadow:** Unlike the Highlights, it consists of the darkest area of an image and allows changes to be made in these areas.
- **Mid-tones:** are areas that are between the darkest and the brightest areas, more like grey. Like the other features, Mid-tones also permit modifications to their areas.

The Dodge Tool

To lighten the area of the image without changing the hue or saturation, use Photoshop's Dodge tool. It can also be used to draw attention to specific elements of the image. If we employ it frequently, saturation will become apparent, turning the dodged parts light grey. Because modifications performed with the dodge tool cannot be reversed, some artists consider it to be "destructive image manipulation."

Options Setting of The Dodge Tool

To effectively use the dodge tools on our artwork, we must be aware of a few crucial characteristics.

The properties of the dodge tool are shown below:

- **Brush Size:** We can adjust the brush's size using this parameter to meet our needs. When you select this option, a pop-up window will appear where you can modify the brush's size and hardness.

Brush Setting: We may give our brushes some extra options by using this attribute. We have many options for our brushes in this brush settings, as the image below demonstrates.

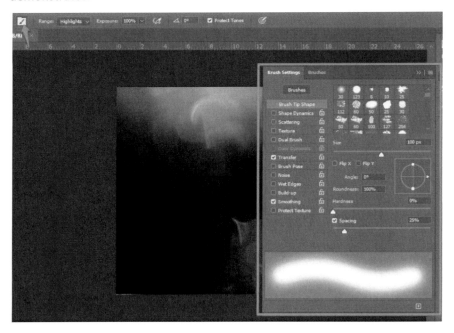

- When you select the range option, a drop-down menu will appear with the following three choices:

  - Mid-tones: This option modifies the grayscale's middle tonal range. It is the range's default choice.
  - Shadows: This setting modifies the image's shadows.
  - Highlights: This choice modifies the image's bright regions.

- **Exposure**: This setting determines how strong the tool's impact will be, similar to how exposed a photo would be. The slider's default value is 50, however it can range from 0 to 100 depending on the situation.

- **Airbrush**: This option is utilized for airbrushes. Choose this option if you wish to utilize an air brush. It will refine your brush.

- **Protect tone**: This option retains the image's tonal quality during lightning, which will stop the colors from shifting in hue.

How Do I use The Dodge Tool?

- Open the image you want to modify in Photoshop
- Choose the dodge tool from the **Tool Bar** but before using it, make a copy of your layer because the dodge tool's effects are irreversible.
- Adjust the tool`s settings in the **Options Bar** to your satisfaction.
- Paint your brush over the region of the image you desire to modify.

The Burn Tool

Usually used in tandem with the Dodge tool, the Burn tool accomplishes essentially the same but opposite results. Here is a description of Burn, its relationship to Dodge, and its advantages.

Burn essentially makes the pixels you paint darker. If used for a long enough period of time, the Burn tool will eventually turn a color completely black, as if you had actually burned it. Burn can be used to create deep shadows.

The Burn Tool is nested with the Dodge and Sponge Tool in The Tool Bar,

The settings for the burn tool are displayed in the **Options Bar.**

The Options Of The Burn Tool

We need to be aware of a few key qualities in order to apply the burn tools on our artwork properly.

- **Brush Size**: Using this parameter, we may change the brush size to suit our requirements. The size and hardness of the brush can be changed in a pop-up box that appears when you choose this option.

◆ **Brush Setting**: By using this attribute, we can provide our brushes with additional options. As the image below shows, we have a lot of options for our brushes in these brush settings.

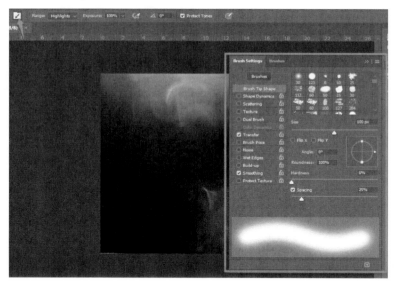

◆ **Range**: The following three options will be available in a drop-down menu when you choose the range option:

- ○ Mid-tones: This setting alters the middle tonal range of the grayscale image. It is the default option for the range.
- ○ Shadows: This option changes the shadows in the image.

○ Highlights: This option changes the bright areas of the image.

✦ **Exposure**: Similar to how exposed a photograph would be, this option influences how powerful the tool's impact will be. The slider can have a value between 0 and 100 depending on the circumstance, with a default value of 50.

✦ **Airbrush**: This choice is used with airbrushes. If an air brush is what you want to use, pick this option. It will make your brush better.

✦ **Protect tone**: This choice prevents color gradation by maintaining the image's tonal quality during lightning.

How do I use The Burn Tool?

✦ Open the image in Photoshop that you wish to edit.
✦ Select the sponge tool from the Tool Bar. Before using the burn tool, make a copy of your layer because its effects are permanent.
✦ Make the necessary adjustments to the tool's parameters in the Options Bar.
✦ Use your brush to paint the area of the image you want to change.

The Sponge Tool

Photoshop's sponge tool affects color saturation. It can either make a hue more saturated or less saturated. This means that by using the sponge tool, we can either make some pixels' colors more intense or make some pixels' colors less intense. The sponge tool is nested with the dodge and burn tool.

The settings of the sponge tool are displayed in the Options Bar in the upper-side of th
Photoshop`s workspace.

When using the sponge tool, the properties bar located beneath the menu bar has tw
modes that must first be understood in order to comprehend how the sponge too
functions:

You can see the two modes in the aforementioned image:

- **Saturate Mode**: This increases the color intensity of the pixels.
- **De-saturate Mode**: This lowers the color intensity of the pixels.

Option Settings of The Sponge Tool

Let's now examine how the sponge tool functions.

- **Brush Preset Picker**: This feature enables us to select the brush type we desire.

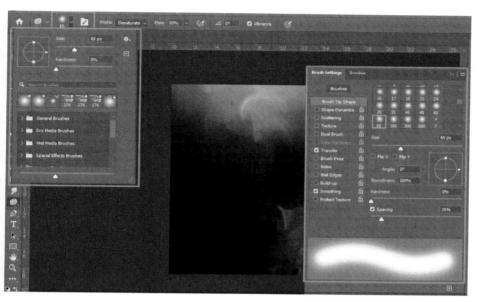

❖ **Mode**: The most significant characteristic of the sponge tool is its mode. The Sponge tool has two modes: Desaturate and Saturate, as we've already covered.

   ○ Desaturate: In this mode, the image's colors are less intense. (That is, it lessens the color's intensity when applied.)

   ○ Saturate: This mode enhances the image's color.

❖ **Flow**: The quantity of saturation or desaturation that will occur when we utilize the sponge tool is determined by this option. Its value range spans 0 and 100%.

❖ **Vibrance**: When this option is selected, the image's vibrancy is maintained while you use the sponge tool. When using the sponge tool, it is essential to keep it under inspection.

- **Pen Pressure Size**: Only users of a graphics tablet are eligible for this feature, which allows for pressure-based brush size adjustment.

How do I use the Sponge Tool?

- Open the image you desire to edit in Photoshop
- From the Tool Bar, choose the sponge tool. Make a copy of your layer before utilizing the sponge tool because its effects are permanent.
- Adjust the tool's settings in the **Options Bar** for the modifications you desire to make.
- Paint the portion of the image you want to edit using your brush.

Other Retouching Tools in Photoshop – Brush Tools

The brush tool, though an actual tool also serves as a nest for other related tools in Photoshop. The Brush tool houses itself, The Pen Tool, Color Replacement Tool and The Mixer Brush Tool.

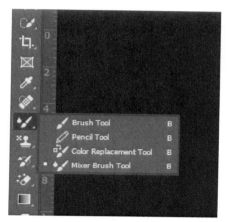

Other brush tools are The History Brush Tool and the Art History Brush Tool, but these tools are nested outside the brush tool.

In this section, we will be studying each of these tools individually and their specific importance to designing and Photography.

The Brush Tool

You can paint on any layer with the Brush tool, just like you would with a real paintbrush. Additionally, there will be a variety of settings available to you, allowing you to tailor it to a variety of circumstances. Once you understand how to use the Brush tool, you'll realize that many other tools, including the Eraser and the Spot Healing Brush, employ a set of parameters that are very similar.

The Brush tool makes it simple to paint in your document. To paint, just click and drag in the document window after finding and selecting the Brush tool from the Tools menu. You can always choose the Brush tool by using the **B** key on your keyboard.

How to use The Brush Tool

- Open a file or picture in Photoshop.
- From the toolbar, pick the Brush tool. As shown in the above image, it may be found on the application's left side.

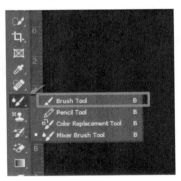

- The Foreground Color, which is the color at the top of the **Color Picker Tool**, should be clicked before selecting a new brush color from the dialog box.

- Adjust your brush settings in the **Options Bar** to your desired taste.

- Simply hold down the left mouse button while dragging the mouse over the image or document after choosing the tool. You only need to press a button for it to begin painting in order to use it.

Options of Brush Tool

We must be aware of a few options the brush tool offers in order to use it effectively in our artwork.

- **Brush Size**: We can adjust the brush's size to suit our demands using this feature of the brush tool. Click the brush picker drop-down button or just right-click the picture or document to alter the brush size. After that, you can either enter the required number in the input box or use the provided slider to change the size of the brush.

  There is a shortcut for changing the brush size, which is to utilize the keyboard's pair of brackets for increasing (]) and decreasing (]). ([ ).

- **Brush Hardness**: Brush hardness refers to the intensity of the brush we use to paint; a harder brush would have sharp edges, whilst a softer brush will have smooth edges. The second slider, titled **Hardness**, can be found in the same drop-down as above. From there, we may adjust the bristles of our brush.

- ♦ **Brush List**: We may also see a list of several brush types in the same drop-down. Photoshop comes with a variety of brushes that we can choose from based on our needs.

- ♦ **Brush Settings**: The symbol for brush settings appears after the brush-picker dropdown icon. Here, we may set up some extra options for our brushes and experiment with them to produce fantastic results for our artwork.

We have a wide variety of options to play with while building up brushes. Here, for instance, we can modify the brush's noise or texture. Additionally, we have a softness slider right here, from which we can only modify the brush's softness.

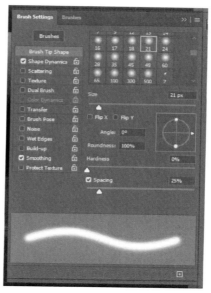

- **Blend Modes**: Blend mode is a huge issue in Photoshop, but we can also access it here in the brush tool choice. Therefore, the main function of blend mode is to alter the mixing of two separate brush strokes. We have a few blending alternatives from which to choose in the blend mode drop-down menu, depending on our needs.

- **Brush Opacity**: Opacity enables us to manage how visible our brushstrokes are. We can adjust the value of the opacity slider from 0% to 100%. Poor opacity indicates low visibility, whereas high opacity indicates high visibility.

- **Brush Flow**: Flow of the brush is yet another crucial aspect of brushes. It simply refers to how much color can flow while painting. To avoid that, we can have a low flow value where the intensity of our color flow will be low and we can have a better outcome. If it is high, more color flows through our brush where it could get messy. Additionally, flow has values ranging from 0% to 100%, or we can utilize slider.

The Pen Tool

A part of brush tools is the pencil tool. With the exception of flow, the pencil tool is simply the tip of a fine, thin brush and has all the same characteristics as a brush.

The Pencil Tool is nested with the brush tool. The shortcut to display the pencil tool is Shift +B. The pencil tool is not a retouching tool but used to make freehand drawings.

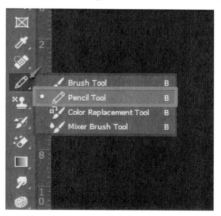

Options Of The Pencil Tool

- **Pencil Size**: The Brush Preset Picker option on the Options Bar displays the tool's default tip size, which is 1 pixel. By clicking the thumbnail or the arrow in the Brush Box, the user can modify the Pencil Brush's tip size.

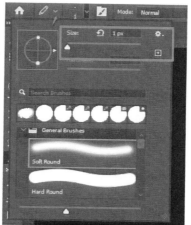

There is a shortcut for changing the brush size, which is to utilize the keyboard's pair of brackets for increasing (]) and decreasing (]). ([ ).

✢ **Brush Hardness**: Brush hardness refers to the intensity of the pencil tip we use to paint; a harder brush would have sharp edges, whilst a softer brush will have smooth edges. The second slider, titled **Hardness**, can be found in the same drop-down as above. From there, we may adjust the bristles of our brush.

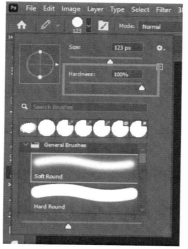

✢ **Brush List**: A drop-down menu may also contain a list of various brush types that we may use for our pencil tool. Depending on our demands, we can choose from a number of brushes that Photoshop includes.

256

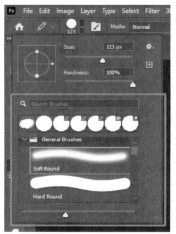

♦ **Brush Settings**: The symbol for brush settings appears after the brush-picker dropdown icon. Here, we may set up some extra options for our brushes and experiment with them to produce fantastic results for our artwork.

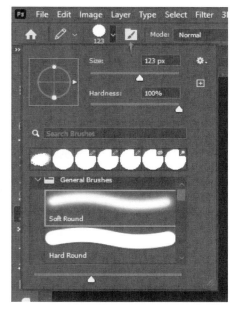

We have a wide variety of options to play with while building up brushes. Here, for instance, we can modify the brush's noise or texture. Additionally, we have a softness slider right here, from which we can only modify the brush's softness.

❖ **Blend Modes**: From the Mode Menu, the user can switch between Blend and Other than Normal Mode. The blend mode enables many methods for blending colors together. The user must modify the brush pencil's mode and opacity on the drawing layer in the Layers Panel. This enables the user to have complete control over the layer and to edit it whenever they want.

- **Brush Opacity**: Opacity enables us to manage how visible our brushstrokes are. We can adjust the value of the opacity slider from 0% to 100%. Poor opacity indicates low visibility, whereas high opacity indicates high visibility.

- **Smoothing**: is an option that influences the brush strokes. If checked, reduces the shakiness of brush strokes.

- **Auto Erase**: draws background color over the foreground color when activated.

How to use The Pencil Tool

- Create a new document if you are not using it on an image or create a new layer for drawing if you are using it on an artwork in Photoshop.
- Select your Pencil tool from the brush tool nest in the Tool Bar
- Adjust the tool`s settings in the Options Bar to meet your specification.
- You can now make freehand drawings with your pencil tool.

Color Replacement Tool

The tool known as a "color replacement" aids in changing any object's or section of a document's color to one of the user's choosing. It is acknowledged as the quickest approach to alter the color of any object, but it also has a drawback in that it is not as precise as other techniques. It is, however, a really simple and user-friendly solution. The color substitution tool's icon or symbol is 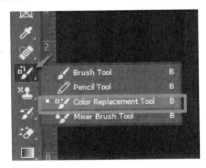. The Color Replacement Tool is nested in the brush tool with other tools in the Tool Bar.

Disadvantages of a color replacement tool:

Although it can swiftly alter the color of the image, it has several accuracy issues and brightness issues. Adjustments -> Hue/Saturation is the method experts use that is more accurate. As a result, the modifications are more exact and color-true. The color replacement tool is still highly advised for newcomers and students learning Photoshop, nevertheless.

Options of the Color Replacement Tool

The color replacement tool icon now displays an option bar with a wide range of possibilities when clicked.

✦ **Brush Size**: The first one (i.e., the one on the far left) is the brush size, where we may adjust the brush's size, hardness, and angle. If you select it, the following dialog box will appear:

- ○ **Size**: To alter the brush's size.
- ○ **Hardness**: To modify the brush's hardness.
- ○ **Spacing**: Increased spacing will result in discontinuous brushstrokes that are spaced apart from one another. (Use only when necessary)
- ○ **Angle**: The brush's angle is modifiable.

- Pen Pressure: Since a graphics tablet is required to view it, it is not utilized here.
- **Mode**: This is one of the color replacement tool's most crucial characteristics. Tools for replacing colors come in four different mode types.
  - Color(Default): This is the color substitution tool's default mode. In this mode, the user's chosen color is simply substituted for the color of the selected area of the image, just like in the article's example.
  - **Hue**: In this option, the hue of the image's selected area is altered.
  - **Saturation**: By changing the color saturation with a less saturated color, this mode can be used to make an image appear dull or bright. By replacing the color saturation with a highly saturated color, this mode can make an image appear bright.
  - **Luminosity**: This setting aids in altering an image's luminosity, or light, to make it bright or dull. Since it frequently degrades the quality of the image, this mode is not recommended for use.

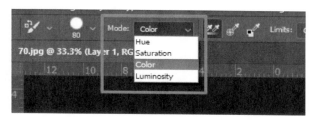

- **Sampling**: The names and descriptions of the three sampling choices are as follows (clockwise from the left):

  - **Continuous Sampling**: With this sampling option, the color replacement tool continuously samples the color as we paint.

- ○ **Once**: In this kind of sampling option, the color replacement tool takes a single sample of the color and then replaces it with the user-selected color wherever it appears.

- ○ **Background**: In this sort of sampling option, the tool substitutes the sampled color for the background color.

- ✦ **Limits**: Limits are the next color substitution choice. This option instructs the color replacement as to how far it may modify the color. Photoshop has three limits mode:

- ○ **Contiguous**: When using this limit option, the tool only changes the color of the pixels in the sampled area that are directly under the cursor. It does not alter the color of the nearby pixels that have the same hue.
- ○ **Dis-contiguous**: With this limit type, the tool modifies the color of the immediate surroundings with a matching sampled color up to the spread of the cursor boundary.
- ○ **Find edges**: In this option, the tool discovers the picture's edges automatically and slows down as we get closer to them, limiting the color change to the edges.
- ✦ **Anti-alias**: Anti-aliasing is the color replacement tool's final feature. Despite the fact that it's not a new tool. It is present in a wide variety of other tools, including erasers and selection tools. Photoshop's anti-alias feature makes it possible to soften the borders of the converted area. Anti-aliasing is turned on by default. Additionally, keeping anti-alias on is advised to provide a perfect color transition at the image's edges.

How do I use The Color Replacement Tool?

✦ Open up your image in Photoshop
✦ Create a selection around the region you want to edit with any selection tool
✦ Select the Color Replacement tool from the Menu Bar

✦ Adjust the tool`s settings in the Options Bar to you desired taste.

✦ Pick the Color you want to replace with from the Color Picker or you pick from the surrounding colors with the eyedropper tool

◆ Apply your brush to replace the colors you desire.

Mixer Brush Tool

Due to its widespread use by digital painters and illustrators, the Mixer Brush tool is also known as "Painter's Paradise." Additionally, photo editors use it in a variety of ways. Skin retouching is one of the mixer brush tool's most crucial applications. Using the mixer brush tool is similar to painting on a real canvas because it simulates using a real paintbrush. The background color and the brush color are blended together. Or, to put it another way, by picking up a sample color from the image you are working on and controlling the rate at which the brush picks up color from the image and the rate at which the paint dries, you can mix colors together as you paint. The brush tool area is where you may find this tool.

In Photoshop, the "Tools" panel is where you can find the Mixer Brush tool. It appears as a paintbrush with a double circle icon 🖌 next to it as the fourth tool from the top in the brush tool nest.

The tool`s settings are displayed on the Options bar in the upper-side of the Photoshop`s workspace.

Options of The Mixer Brush Tool

It becomes a very potent instrument with the aid of these alternatives. The mixer brush tool's choice bar appears when we pick it, as illustrated below:

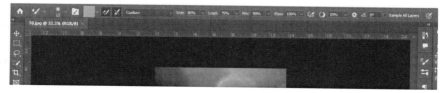

264

- **Brush Size**: Each brush tool has the same option. We can change the brush's size, angle, and sharpness with this option.

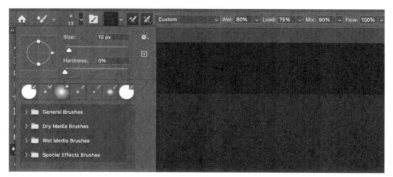

- **Current Brush Load**: This choice displays the brush's loaded color at the moment. This choice now comes with intriguing features. If we click on it, further alternatives, as listed below, become available.

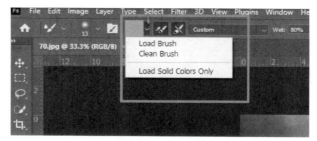

  - ○ **Load Brush**: Reload the brush with color using the load option.
  - ○ **Clean Brush**: This choice cleans the brush.
  - ○ **Load Solid Color Only**: When the box labeled "Load Solid Color Only" is selected, the brush will only load solid colors.
    The question of whether the brush can select anything other than the solid color may now be raised. True is the response.
- **Load the brush after each stroke**: The brush will automatically reload with the same color after each stroke if this option is left checked.

- **Clean the brush after each stroke**: The brush will automatically clean itself after each stroke if this option is left checked.

- **Presets**: These options have a number of pre-defined functions that were created by setting various Wet, load, and mix values. It is set to custom by default, allowing us to create our own preset. You will see something similar if you select the option:

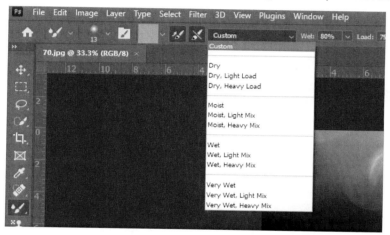

- **Wet**: The value of this option falls between 0 and 100%. This option lets us know how much paint the brush picks up from the canvas, and when we set the wet value to greater than zero, the mix option is also active. Less wet and more mix equals less color that will blend.

- **Load**: This option also has a value that falls between 0 and 100%. This option displays the amount of paint that is currently on our brush. The more the value, the more paint is on the brush. As with a real brush, the color load depletes as we

266

paint with it. We get a brush that looks like a typical paintbrush if we set the load to 100% and the Wet and Mix settings to 0.

♦ **Mix**: This option also has a value that falls between 0 and 100%. The amount of color mixing with the colors of the canvas when we paint with a brush is indicated by this option. We already know that if wet is set to 0, the brush won't pick up any color, so this option is only enabled when wet has a value greater than 0.

♦ **Flow**: This option also has a value that falls between 0 and 100%. This setting regulates how quickly the color flows throughout each stroke. More color is produced during the stroke with a higher flow rate. The flow is set to 100% by default.

♦ **Smoothing**: The amount by which it will lessen the shakiness in the brush stroke depends on the value that is selected.

♦ **Sample All layers**: The brush will act as if it is painting on a single layer of canvas even if there may be multiple layers if this option is checked. The tool merges all the layers into one and paints with it even though it has several layers. The option to sample all layers is always selected by default.

How do I use the Mixer Brush Tool?

As was already mentioned, the background color and brush color are combined using the mixer brush tool. Let's now examine this in greater detail.

- Open a new document of Adobe Photoshop
- Use the regular brush tool to paint a part of the document with any color of your choice.

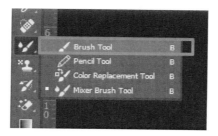

- Select the Mixer Brush from the Tool Menu

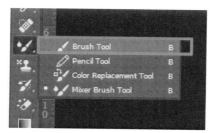

- Adjust the brush`s settings in the Options bar if necessary.

✦ Select a new color from the Color picker now (different from the color that you have previously chosen).

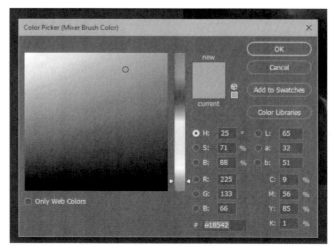

✦ Simply paint over the previous painting and you will get the result of using the mixer brush tool.

History Brush Tool

The History Brush tool allows you to restore parts of an image to an earlier history state by painting over them. In other to use the history brush effectively, you must understand how the History panel affects its functions.

The History Panel in Photoshop

A panel in Photoshop called the History Panel displays a history or log of all the operations carried out on the current Photoshop file since its inception. The history panel can be accessed via the **Window menu** => **History** or from the right side of the documents, as demonstrated below.

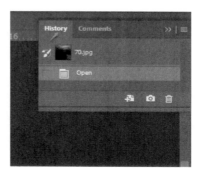

The history panel, as you can see from the image above, displays all the alterations and work that have been made to the current Photoshop file. The snapshot button is a tiny icon that is highlighted in red in the above image. This option enables us to take a screenshot of a Photoshop document at a specific time during the entire session. If something goes wrong or is damaged, the user can pick a point from which to resume work rather than having to start at the beginning.

Using The History Brush Tool

So now we are aware of what the history panel is. We'll now cover how to employ the History brush tool. The history brush tool will be ineffective if you don`t have a log of history of works on your image.

 ✦ Open the Photoshop file for the image.
 ✦ After making changes to your image and you desire to return a region of the image to its default mode, select the History brush tool from the Tool Menu on the left side of Photoshop`s workspace.

↕ When you want to go back in history to the initial default image, you will see that the cursor has been changed to a brush. Simply brush over the desired areas.

Properties of The History Brush Tool

The properties/settings of the history brush tool are displayed on the Options bar like every other tool in Photoshop.

We can see a lot of properties here. Let's now examine each of these characteristics individually.

Note: In Adobe Photoshop, the History Brush tool's settings are identical to those of the Normal Brush tool.

↕ **Mode**: This sets the brush's mode; we can choose from a variety of modes by selecting the mode option, as illustrated below:

Normal is the mode's default setting. You can choose modes based on your needs

↕ **Opacity**: The opacity controls how opaque the brush is. Its value falls between 0 and 100%. The brush's opacity is set to 100% by default.

271

♦ **Flow**: The brush effect's flow is determined by the flow (color in the case of the normal brush).

♦ **Pressure Control Size**: This choice is only applicable if you're using a graphics tablet with adjustable pressure. if you have this option turned on and you're using a graphics tablet. The size of your brush will then adjust based on how hard you press on the tablet.

The Art History Brush Tool

An interesting alternative to the standard History Brush tool is the Art History Brush tool in Adobe Photoshop. Both Tools reuse data from a prior state to paint over an image. However, the Art History Brush tool offers a variety of options on the Options bar that let you add a brush-stroke appearance to your painting. The Art History brush is nested with the History brush tool in the Tool Menu.

ption Settings of the Art History Brush Tool

272

This feature of the art history brush tool is displayed on the Options bar like every other tool in Photoshop.

♦ The brush settings in this tool are similar to that of a regular brush.

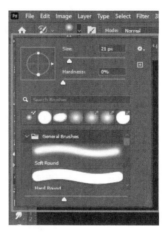

♦ **Mode**: This determines the brush's mode; by selecting the mode option, as seen below, we can select from several options.

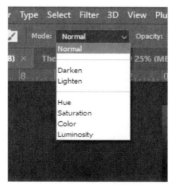

♦ **Style**: Different-shaped brush stroke designs, such as Tight short, Loose Medium, Dab, or Loose Curl, etc. are available in the Style menu.

273

- **Area**: Independent of the brush size you choose, this selection determines the area that the paint stroke covers. Greater area coverage is achieved with larger brush sizes.

- **Tolerance**: With this option, you may change how much of a change is made to your photo. You can apply strokes wherever in the image, regardless of the color values, by using a lower tolerance value. A high tolerance number restricts Art History strokes to areas that are significantly different from the source state or image, resulting in a far less pronounced difference between your image and the original.

- **Opacity**: determines the transparency of the brush you are drawing with.

Working with The Eraser Tool

Since Photoshop contains so many tools, it might be difficult to know which one to use to achieve a certain effect or task. You've probably questioned a little bit about the tiny eraser in your toolbar after seeing it. Photoshop's Eraser Tool has some uses, but it also has some drawbacks.

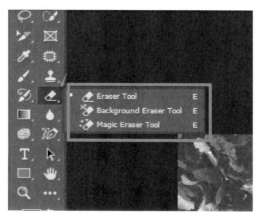

The Eraser, **Background Eraser**, and **Magic Eraser** are the three options available when using the Eraser tool. Using the Pencil has an auto-erase feature as well.

But it's crucial to remember that the Eraser tool is destructive. That implies that any time you use the Eraser tool, your work is irreversible. The only way to get it back is to repeatedly instruct Photoshop to "Undo." You'll probably have to start over if you detect your error after you've already saved. Consider the Eraser tool to be a traditional eraser. In the actual world, if you wipe something, it's gone.

If you don't want to work destructively, you might be wondering how to get rid of items from your image that you don't want. To change a layer, simply add a layer mask to it, then use the Brush tool to mask.

Although the Eraser tool appears useful, you can accomplish the same tasks more quickly and effectively with a layer mask, for example. If you intend to continue using the Eraser tool, you must duplicate the layer you're working on in case you need to start over.

Follow the procedure below to use the eraser tool effectively,

- Open the image you want to modify in Photoshop. By default, your opened image appears locked in the background layer.

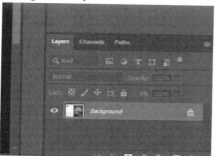

- If you desire to use your eraser tool on the image while it is still locked unless you unlock the background layer, it will appear like you are painting with ground color while you think you are erasing. To reveal the checkerboard pattern underneath, unlock your layer so that it can be hidden.
- If the image you are working on is a smart object. The eraser tool can`t work on it until it is rasterized.
- Once everything above has been sorted, depending on the effect you want, choose between the **brush**, **pencil**, and **block** modes. Blocks are square with hard edges, whereas pencils have more of a drawn-line appearance, and brushes have rounded, soft edges.

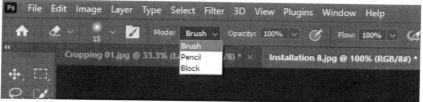

- In the settings **Option bar**, you must configure the **opacity** and **flow** when using the brush or pencil modes. Opacity describes the degree of erasure you desire for the pixels. For instance, opacity at 100% will fully remove images while opacity at lower levels will only partially do so.

Erase to History: This option in the option bar erases area options designated states.

276

- Drag the cursor across the areas you want to remove while keeping it down.

In essence, the Eraser tool is a brush. Like with any brush, you can alter the size, hardness, and spacing. Additionally, you have the option of switching the mode from Brush to Penci or Block. The Eraser, however, removes the undesirable pixels from your image rather than painting on them. Those pixels have been permanently deleted and may only be restored by selecting "Undo."

Follow the procedures below, to use the **background eraser tool** effectively,

- Select the layer containing the regions you want to remove from the Layers panel
- When the option appears, keep holding down the Eraser tool and select Background Eraser.

- Select a brush and alter the size, hardness, angle, roundness, and spacing settings.
- Choose the **Limits mode**
    - o **Discontiguous**: Wherever the sampled color appears beneath the brush, discontiguous removes it.
    - o **Contiguous** eliminates sampling color in related areas.
    - o With **Find Edges**, related regions that have the sample color are removed while edges' shapes are preserved.

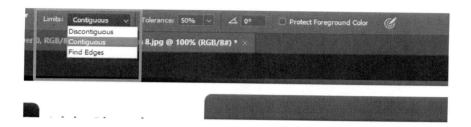

❖ **Tolerance level** can be chosen by dragging the slider. Compared to low tolerance, which looks for colors that are extremely similar to the sample color, high tolerance will delete a larger spectrum of hues.

❖ To prevent accidentally removing the foreground colors, choose **Protect Foreground Color.**

❖ Decide on a sampling strategy
  ○ If you choose Continuous, the eraser tool will continuously sample colors while you are dragging it
  ○ Only the color you first click on will be erased.
  ○ Any spots that contain the background color will be removed by Background Swatch.

he Eraser tool is distinct from the Background Eraser tool. The tool and cursor will switch ɔ a circle with a + in the center as soon as you click. By default, the Background Eraser tool samples the color that lies just beneath the + in the circle's center. Photoshop will therefore remove all of that color from the broader circle.

The **Background Eraser options** are shown below,

* The first choice is to alter the "brush's" size.
* You can select whether you want the Background Eraser to operate **continuously**, **once**, or through a **swatch** using the second option, which begins with two eyedroppers and a gradient below.
    * o The word "**continuous**" was used in the dog photo. When attempting to remove a backdrop with multiple colors, the continuous option performs well.
    * o When you click **once**, the color will be erased as instructed. The color that Photoshop knows to save and remove when you start rotating the circle around the image is where the + is when you click.
    * o With the Tools palette's **Background swatch** option, you can specify a background color that the Background Eraser will only remove.
* The Limits section is the next one, and it offers the **Contiguous**, Discontiguous, and **Find Edges options**
    * o **Contiguous**: Only pixels near the pixel beneath the + will be erased by contiguous. The Contiguous option can be annoying if you need to remove something that has obstacles, like hair or branches.
    * o Even if they are not in the same region as the +, the **Discontiguous** option will remove all pixels that match the color you are erasing.
    * o **Find Edges** performs exactly what its name implies; it erases up to the edges that it discovers.
* The Background Eraser settings continue with a section called **Tolerance.** Simply put, the more variants of the sampled color Photoshop will obliterate, the greater the Tolerance setting. You'll need a low Tolerance if the color of your background is comparable to the object you don't want to remove. Starting lower and working your way up is a solid strategy in any case.
* When you choose **Protect Foreground Color** from the Tools palette, Photoshop will shield the foreground color from erasure. The Protect Foreground Color

checkbox should be selected if the object you're seeking to protect is almost identical to the backdrop but somewhat dissimilar in color.

Follow the procedures below, to use the **Magic Eraser tool**.

✦ The Magic Eraser tool is selected from the toolbar

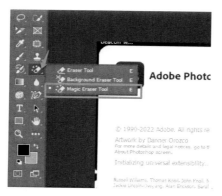

✦ Select a tolerance number. Low tolerance just erases colors that are comparable to the one you've chosen, whereas high tolerance erases a wide range of colors.

✦ If you want sharp edges, choose Anti-Aliased.

✦ Depending on whether you want to delete only adjacent pixels or all similar pixels, choose or deselect **Contiguous**.

✦ To view a sample of the color that was wiped from visible layers, select Sample All Layers.

- Select and modify Opacity.

- To delete a portion of the layer, click the desired area.

The Magic Eraser tool functions similarly to the Magic Wand tool in that a larger region i selected based on pixel contrast. Using the Magic Wand tool and then pressing delete i exactly how the Magic Eraser operates. The Magic Eraser appears to be simple to use Photoshop will automatically delete all the pixels in that area that are that color whe you simply click where you want to remove anything.

CHAPTER TEN

FILTERS IN PHOTOSHOP

What you will learn in this chapter.

- **What Photoshop Filters are.**
- **How to use the amazing filters in Photoshop; Extended Filters, Filter Gallery, Adaptive Wide Angle, Camera Raw Filter, Lens Correction, Liquify, Vanishing Point.**
- **How to use Artistic Filters, Blur Filters, Blur Gallery Filters, Brush Strokes Filters, Distort Filters, Noise Filters, Pixelate Filters, Render Filters, Stylize Filters, Sharpen Filters, Video Filters and Other Filters**

Introduction to Photoshop Filters

The Photoshop filter is one of Adobe's most important tools; it can add unique effects to an image and completely alter its feel and style. It is primarily used by expert photographers, graphic designers, and photo editors to reduce distortions and enhance image quality. Furthermore, amateurs and hobbyists use it for their projects. There are numerous third-party filters on the internet, most of which are accessible as plug-ins. However, the software itself provides a range of filters that you can use to suit your needs.

You can quickly change the contents of layers using Photoshop filters. They include basic effects like image sharpening and stylization (e.g., adding a glow to the edges or creating a craquelure effect). Certain filters enable more intricate effects, such as adjusting the image's pixel placement or applying a high-pass filter.

The active layer or the layer mask of the active selection is affected by filters. If there is no selection, the filter is applied to the layer as a whole or the layer mask.

By adding Smart Filters to Smart Objects, you can use filters without causing any harm. Smart Filters can be updated at any time using the original image data that is stored in the Smart Object. In the Layers panel, Smart Filters are stored as layer effects. For more information about smart filter effects and nondestructive editing.

Select the relevant submenu command from the Filter menu to employ a filter. You can choose filters with the aid of these recommendations:

- Filters are applied to a selection of the currently active, visible layer.
- Most filters can be applied cumulatively on photos with 8 bits per channel using the Filter Gallery. Each filter may be used independently.

- Bitmap-mode or indexed-color images cannot be subjected to filters.
- Certain filters only function on RGB photos.
- 8-bit images can be processed with any filter.
- For 16-bit images, the following filters can be used: Liquify, Vanishing Poi Average Blur, Blur, Blur More, Box Blur, Gaussian Blur, Lens Blur, Motion Bl Radial Blur, Surface Blur, Shape Blur, Lens Correction, Add Noise, Despeckle, Du & Scratches, Median, Reduce Noise, Fibers, Clouds, Difference Clouds, Lens Fla Sharpen, Sharpen Edges, Sharpen More,
- For use on 32-bit photos, the following filters are available: Add Noise, Clouds, Le Flare, Smart Sharpen, Unsharp Mask, De-Interlace, NTSC Colors, Emboss, Hi Pass, Maximum, Minimum, and Offset.
- Some filters are completely processed in RAM. A notification may appear if the isn't enough RAM available to process a filter effect.

The Menu where all filters are nested in the **Filter Menu** in the **Menu bar.**

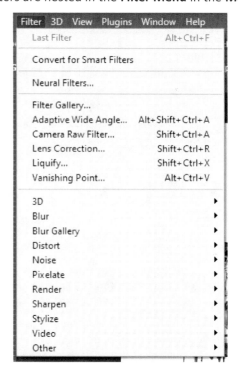

Knowing How to use Filters in Photoshop

In the Filter Menu are various filters, while some are grouped. Some aren't. **Extended filters** and **Filter Gallery** are the two groups of filters in Photoshop while others exist individually.

Extended Filters

The additional filters known as extended filters do not fall under another category. These are more recent filters with sophisticated pixel analysis, calculations, and filter effect groups.

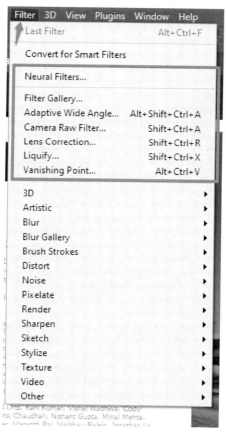

Extended Filters include Neural Filters, Filter Gallery, Adaptive Wide Angle, Camera Raw Filter, Lens Correction, Liquify, and Vanishing Point.

Using The Neural Filters

Neural filters are an easy and fun way to make visually striking changes and speed up your image editing processes. You can find them under the Filters tab in Adobe Photoshop. Using algorithms, Neural Filters—which are driven by Adobe Sensei's machine learning and artificial intelligence engine—create new pixels in your photos. You can quickly test out fresh, imaginative concepts and make nondestructive adjustments while preserving the integrity of the original image by doing this.

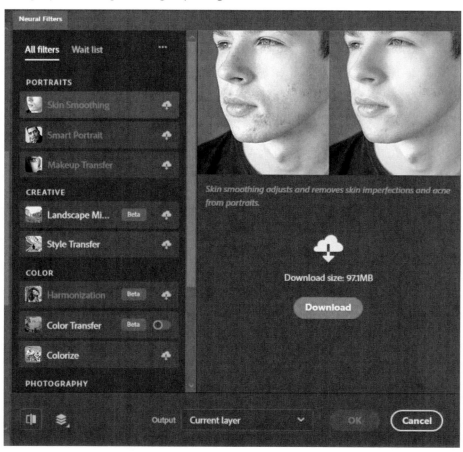

In the Neural Filters, Photoshop has five pre-installed featured filters that are available for usage as soon as you open your image. Choose one to improve your shot, or experiment with them all to find one that suits you the best.

- **Skin Smoothing**: The Skin Smoothing filter makes it simple to brush and adjust the skin of your subjects. You may quickly remove tattoos, freckles, scars, and other characteristics from faces and skin using the straightforward Smoothness and Blur sliders.

✦ **Smart Portraits**: With the movable sliders in this filter, you may alter the facial age, posture, expressions, and any other minute features of your subject. Create and alter masks that you can apply to your subject to make modest aesthetic adjustments or even to create weird emotions. Keep the distinguishing characteristics of your topic despite all the alterations by using the Retain Unique Details slider.

✦ **Makeup Transfer**: Use this helpful tool to apply the same cosmetics settings to numerous faces. To achieve the ideal look for your photograph, add additional cosmetics to a photo or entirely alter the model's existing makeup in post-production.

✦ **Landscape Mixer**: Create completely original landscapes by combining the best elements of two photos. Start with your landscape image, then pick a landscape reference image. To produce a new image, Landscape Mixer will combine elements from the two images. To alter how the time of day and season seem, use the Winter, Spring, Summer, Fall, and Sunset sliders.

✦ **Style Transfer**: With this filter, you can apply the color, hue, or saturation of one image to another, exactly as its name implies. You may control how much of the final appearance your image has by adjusting the sliders for Style Strength, Brush Size, and Blur Background as well as checking boxes for Preserve Color and Focus Subject.

✦ **Harmonization**: The Harmonization filter adds the color and tone of your reference image to any layer. Enjoy the symmetry of the colors as you adjust the sliders and add a mask.

✦ **Color Transfer**: In a matter of seconds, stunning colors flow seamlessly from one image to the next. Apply the color scheme from any reference image onto the photo of your choice by using Color Transfer. Play around with the countless reference photo options, try out different color moods, and give old pictures a fresh look.

✦ **Colorize**: Transform photos from black and white to vibrant colors in a flash. Choose the colors you wish to see in your capture, and Adobe Sensei will fill the picture with those colors. To fine-tune the filter, focus points enable you to add more color to particular regions.

✦ **Super Zoom**: Focus tightly on a subject while maintaining clarity of details. To allow your subject (whatever it is) to shine through in an extreme close-up, enhance facial characteristics, minimize noise, and remove compression artifacts.

- **Depth Blur**: Your picture will automatically be hazy. Mask out the foreground, add some haze, and make the necessary adjustments. To adjust the quantity of haze, as well as its color temperature, hue, saturation, and other factors, use the preset sliders in Photoshop.
- **JPEG Artifacts Removal**: Your image is more likely to seem pixelated or fuzzy the more times you save a JPEG file. Due to the compression technologies employed to minimize the file size, artifacts (obvious visual irregularities) may be seen. With this filter, you may reverse the process and fine-tune it by changing the blur level at the image's edge from high to medium to low.
- **Photo Restoration**: Photoshop Beta has a feature for photo restoration. It was revealed by Adobe in June 2022. It uses a new AI-powered Neural Filter to recover old or damaged photographs. You can further hone them by utilizing additional changes or basic editing options. Each of these sliders is simple to operate.

Filter Gallery

You can examine a preview of how an image will appear after you apply a certain filter to it in the Filter Gallery. You may preview the effect through the gallery rather than having to apply a lot of filters one at a time to an image.

Before you click on a filter to view a preview, you can also see an icon of what the filter does in addition to being able to see how it will appear when applied to your image. This can speed up and simplify the process of discovering a filter or the particular kind of filter you're looking for. When you're in the Filter Gallery, you may also edit the filter's settings and then apply them to your image.

Adaptive Wide Angle

Use an adaptive wide angle filter to correct lens distortions caused by using wide angle lenses. You can easily straighten lines that appear curved in panoramas and images taken with fish-eye and wide-angle lenses. When taken with a wide-angle lens, buildings, for example, seem to be leaning inward.

Once the filter has identified the camera and lens models, it uses the lens characteristics to align the images. Set multiple constraints to draw attention to straight lines in different parts of the image. With this understanding, the Adaptive Wide Angle filter removes the distortions.

You can also use this filter on images without camera and lens information, though it will take a bit more effort. If you want to change the filter settings later, convert the layer to a smart object.

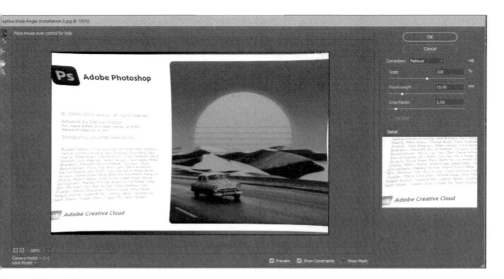

Camera Raw Filter

Camera Raw was originally an Adobe Bridge plug-in that let photographers work on their raw photos without having to shell out a lot of cash for expensive editing programs. Since then, Lightroom's image processing features have been built upon Camera Raw, which has developed into a potent image editor in and of itself. Since Photoshop CC's initial release, users have also had the option to utilize Camera Raw as a filter on RGB or greyscale images instead of more popular image adjustments like Curves or Hue/Saturation.

Only grayscale or RGB images with a pixel count of no more than 65,000 in eithe dimension may be processed with the Camera Raw filter.

In Photoshop, choose the Camera Raw Filter option from the Filter menu by hitting the Command + Shift + A keyboard shortcut on Mac or the Control + Shift + A keyboard shortcut on PC. Using Camera Raw to convert an image into a Smart Object (Smart Filter layer allows you to apply adjustments without affecting the original.

This lets you adjust the Camera Raw settings, just as you would when working on a raw image. Certain workflows might benefit from this. When working with scanned photos for example, capture sharpening can be applied using the Camera Raw filter. Maybe you'l be more comfortable using the Camera Raw Basic panel controls for tone-editing ar image instead of Levels or Curves.

Another benefit is that you can apply additional Camera Raw-specific adjustments, like using Clarity to adjust the mid-tone contrast or doing black-and-white conversions in the Camera Raw style.

Lens Correction

Typical lens flaws such as barrel and Pincushion distortion, vignetting, and chromatic aberration are corrected by the Lens Correction filter. The filter works only with 8- anc 16-bit-per-channel images in grayscale or RGB mode.

In addition, the filter can be used to rotate a picture and fix perspective problems resulting from a horizontal or vertical camera tilt. These adjustments are easier and more accurate to make with the filter's picture grid than with the Transform command.

There are two ways to use Photoshop Lens Correction. Alternatively, you can let Photoshop handle the repairs on its own. The problem is that you are powerless over the circumstances. Thus, the manual method is an option.

Liquify

One of Photoshop's most effective tools for editing and repairing photos is the liquify tool. With it, you can quickly address issues like wrinkling or distortion, or you can go beyond straightforward adjustments to produce entirely new effects.

Simply choose the "liquify" tool from the toolbar to begin altering. You can personalize the impact to acquire the outcomes you desire because there are several possibilities available. For later usage, you may also save your settings as a preset.

Use the liquify tool to experiment with your photographs and produce one-of-a-kind, eye-catching effects. Try it out and see what you can think of!

Vanishing Point

In photos that incorporate perspective planes, such as the sides of a building, walls, floors, or any rectangular object, Vanishing Point makes perspective-correct editing easier. You define the planes in an image with Vanishing Point before making adjustments like painting, cloning, copying or pasting, and transforming. Every adjustment you make respects the viewpoint of the plane you're working on. Because the changes are correctly oriented and scaled to the perspective planes, the results are more realistic whether you retouch, add, or delete content from an image. You can carry on modifying the image in Photoshop once you've finished your work in Vanishing Point. Save your project in the PSD, TIFF, or JPEG formats if you want to keep the perspective plane information in a picture.

Let`s quickly examine some of the other filters in the Filer menu.

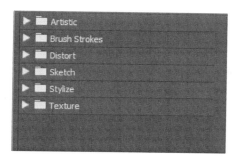

Artistic Filter

These filter effects give images a painted or artistic appearance by mimicking the look of natural or traditional media. Artistically applied filters produce imaginative painted-art images by combining color, brushstrokes, and textures. It works well and is primarily employed in commercial or fine art projects.

Artistic Filters include **Colored Pencils**, **Cutouts**, **Dry Brush**, **Film Grain**, **Fresco**, **Neon Glow**, **Paint Daubs**, **Palette Knife**, **Plastic Wrap**, **Poster Edges**, **Rough Pastels**, **Smudge Stick**, **Sponge**, **Underpainting**, and **Watercolor**.

- **Colored Pencil**: The use of pencil colors on a solid background gives the images in this effect a rough crosshatch appearance.
- **Cutout**: This option creates an image that exactly resembles the rough-cut bits of colorful paper.
- **Dry Brush**: By limiting its color range to the common color areas, this function gives a dry brush appearance when painting the image's edges.

- **Film Grain**: It can get rid of blend banding and give the shadow tones and mid-tones a more saturated pattern.
- **Smudge Stick**: To soften the darker parts, try applying short diagonal strokes. It can lose detail when applied to lighter areas.
- **Neon Glow**: This option allows you to colorize and soften an image by adding several kinds of lights to it.
- **Palette Knife**: By reducing the visual details, you can create the appearance of a canvas that has been lightly painted.
- **Watercolor**: With this option, the photographs will have a watercolor effect thanks to a medium brush that has been loaded with color and water.
- **Paint Daubs**: The photographs have a painted appearance and users can choose from a variety of brush sizes and types.
- **Plastic Wrap**: For accentuating the surface detail of the image, it creates the appearance of a liquid or slick plastic coating.

Blur Filters

It is a set of filters that are mostly used for photo editing. It can be applied to a particular area of the image or the whole thing. Furthermore, you can choose the desired blur type and degree. Blur filters apply a range of distinct blur effects by averaging color, direction, and distance. These can soften and defocus the image while removing unwanted roughness, noise, and dust. They can also be used to blend in newly added background objects.

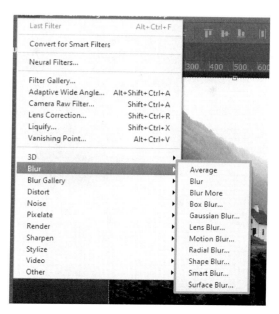

❖ **Average**: It will assist you in locating images or selections with average colors so that you can fill them with the preferred hue to give them a smoother appearance.

❖ **Movement Blur**: To enhance realistic motion effects, it is employed. This effect, for instance, can provide the impression that a moving object with a set time exposure is present in an image.

❖ **Shape Blur**: A kernel, which can be selected from a list of shape presets, is used to create the blur. Use the radius slider to change its size.

❖ **Surface Blur**: This filter option allows you to blur an image while keeping the image's edges sharp. Typically, it is employed to clean up the images' noise and grain.

❖ **Lens blur**: This filter gives the appearance of a smaller field of view, focusing attention on the key elements in the image while blurring the background.

❖ **Gaussian Blur**: It provides a configurable amount of blurriness or haze to the chosen area of the image. Additionally, it offers a low-frequency detail.

❖ **Radial Blur**: By choosing the Spin option and then deciding how far to rotate the camera, you may add a gentle blur to a zoomed-out or spinning image.

❖ **Smart Blur**: Once you've chosen the ideal threshold, radius, and blur quality, this filter option will allow you to blur the image precisely.

Blur Gallery Filters

Further development of the blur filters, the Blur Gallery Filters offer more complex specialized blur shapes and uses. These can imitate regular camera lenses and create blur along a path. All five Blur Gallery filters can be used simultaneously by dragging the checkmarks next to them on the right side of the screen.

Included in the Blur Gallery Filters are Field, Iris, Tilt-Shift, Path, and Spin blur filters.

Brush Strokes Filters

Several brush and pen stroke effects are included to enhance the visuals' aesthetic appeal. With the brush stroke filters, you can add a range of effects to the photos, such as paint, noise, texture, and edge detail. Brush stroke filters mimic traditional paintbrushes and painting techniques by using color, line, and texture.

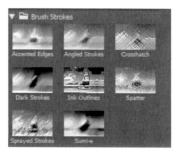

Brush Strokes Filters include Accented Edges, Angled Strokes, Crosshatch, Dark Strokes, Ink Outlines, Spatter, Sprayed Strokes, and Sumi-e

- **Splatter**: This result is comparable to the splatter airbrush effect, which can be utilized to streamline the image's overall effects.
- **Dark Strokes**: You'll be able to paint the lighter sections efficiently with long, white strokes and the darker areas effectively with short, dark strokes.
- **Sprayed Strokes**: By using sprayed and angular strokes using Sprayed, you can repaint a picture using dominant colors.
- **Angles Strokes**: By using sprayed and angular strokes using Sprayed, you can repaint a picture using dominant colors.
- **Crosshatch**: By including approximated pencil hatching, it helps to add texture and roughen the borders of colored sections of an image.

Distort Filters

Distortion filters are used to move, compress, and stretch the pixels to create a variety of effects. To function, these often require more computer memory.

Distort Filters include Diffuse Glow, Displace, Glass, Ocean Ripple, Pinch, Polar Coordinates, Ripple, Shear, Spherize, Twirl, Wave, and ZigZag.

- **Spherize**: By warping the image or selection and bending it to fit the curve, it will create the illusion of three dimensions.
- **ZigZag**: To accurately distort the selected part of the image, you must specify the radius of the pixel and comprehend how to move it.
- **Ripple**: In this situation, you must define the dimensions and quantity of ripples based on which an undulating pattern will be produced in the specified area.
- **Ocean Ripple**: Using it, you can add irregularly spaced ripples to the picture's surface to give the impression that it is underwater.

✦ **Glass**: This effect gives the impression that you are wearing various types of glasses to watch the image. You can apply it or make your glass effect.

✦ **Displace**: With this effect, the image appears to be seen through several types of glasses. You can utilize it or make your customized glass effect to apply

Noise Filters

To produce an image or texture that is more uniform, noise filters either add or remove noise (random color or brightness of image pixels).

✦ **Reduce Noise**: By lowering the noise and maintaining the edges, it will have an impact on the image as a whole or the specific choices.

✦ **Add Noise**: You may give photographs that have been heavily edited a realistic appearance by adding ransom pixels.

✦ **Dust & Scratches**: In this situation, you can lessen the noise and strike a balance between intensifying the image and hiding imperfections.

✦ **Median**: To lessen noise, it combines the pixel brightness inside the selection. The filter can also be used to lessen motion effects.

Pixelate Filters

Using these sets of filters, cells with similar color pixels are grouped to define a selection. To make patterns and effects, Pixelate Filters group colors.

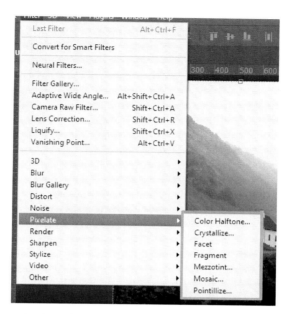

- **Color Halftone**: It gives the impression that the image is divided into rectangles and then replaced on each channel of a bigger halftone screen.
- **Facet**: When this effect is present, solid or similar-colored pixels will cluster together to form blocks of the same color. It is typically employed to give the scanned image a hand-painted appearance.
- **Mezzotint**: Using this filter, you can change a normal image into a random black-and-white pattern or highly saturated hues into a color image.
- **Pointillize**: In this type of effect, you can disperse the colors of the image into haphazardly scattered dots, much like in a pointillist painting.

Render Filters

Numerous 3D shapes, such as spherical, cubical, and cylindrical shapes, as well as different cloud patterns, lighting effects, and refraction and reflection patterns, can be produced with this filter. Render filters create new images that can be used to replace or combine with existing ones.

Flame, Picture Frame, Tree, Clouds, Difference Clouds, Fibres, Lens Flare, and Lighting Effects (Deprecated (3D)) are examples of render filters.

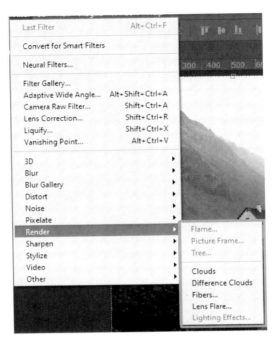

✦ **Clouds**: By utilizing random values that fluctuate between background and foreground colors, it is possible to produce a gentle cloud pattern.

✦ **Lighting Effects**: By adjusting various styles, types, and characteristics, you can use this filter to generate an infinite number of lighting effects on RGB photographs.

✦ **Fibers**: This filter uses the color of the foreground and background to simulate woven fibers in the image.

✦ **Lens flare**: In this situation, shining a strong light through the camera lens will make it appear as though there is refraction occurring inside the image.

Stylize Filters

This effect will cause the pixels to shift and the contrast to increase, giving the image selection a painted look. Stylize Filters add depth, height, and line effects to create dynamic embossing and line-art effects.

Diffuse, Emboss, Extrude, Find Edges, Glowing Edges, Oil Paint, Solarize, Tiles, Trace Contour, and Wind are examples of stylize filters.

✦ **Diffuse**: By rearranging the pixels in the selection by various settings like normal, lighten only, darken only, etc., you can use it to soften the focus.

✦ **Wind**: The photographs can have a wind-blown appearance thanks to this filter. It offers many options including Wind, Blast, and Stagger.

✦ **Find Edges**: This effect will highlight the edges of the image and assist you in locating the specific areas of the image that have undergone various alterations.

✦ **Tiles**: The image can be divided into a sequence of tiles, with the space between each tile able to be filled with a variety of alternatives, including the reversed image, the foreground color, the background color, the original image, etc.

✦ **Glowing Edges**: This technique may be used cumulatively by locating the color edges of the photos and incorporating a neon-like glow into them.

Sharpen Filters

Sharpen filters employ contrast to enhance the edges of photos, resulting in more distinct lines and separation and a clearer, sharper image.

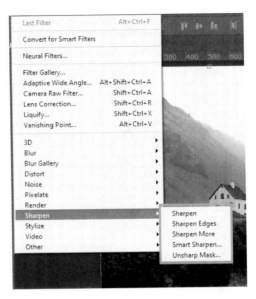

Sharpen Filters include Sharpen, Sharpen Edges, Sharpen More, Smart Sharpen, and Unsharp Mask.

Video Filters

Frames from or for videos are processed using video filters.

Video Filters include De-Interlace and NTSC Colors.

Other Filters

By choosing "Others" from this sub-menu, you can adjust the picture masks, balance the image selection, adjust the colors, and create custom filters. Other Filters can be used to quickly move and change pixels in addition to creating custom filters.

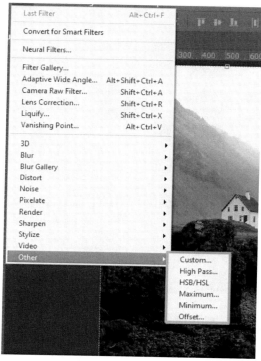

Other Filters include Custom, High Pass, HSB/HSL, Material Filter, Maximum, Minimum, and Offset

Maximum and Minimum: These are used to modify masks. The "Maximum" filter will give the effect of a spread whereas the "Minimum" filter will give the effect of a choke.

Custom: Using this option, you can customize your effect and adjust the brightness of each pixel according to convolution, that is, a predefined mathematical operation.

High Pass: This effect will help you retain the image edges according to the specified radius while allowing you to conceal the rest. It`s just the opposite of the Gaussian blur.

CHAPTER ELEVEN

TIPS AND TRICKS ON PHOTOSHOP 2024

What you will learn in this chapter.

- How to change settings in Photoshop using the Preference Window.
- Shortcuts for blending modes.
- How save and loads selections in Photoshop.
- Popular shortcuts in Photoshop.
- Shortcuts for selection tools.
- Function Keys Shortcuts
- Shortcuts for viewing images.
- Shortcuts for selecting and moving objects.
- Shortcuts for selecting and editing texts

Tips and Tricks

We'll go over some practical Photoshop tips and tricks in this section. Many Photoshop hints and techniques are offered to foster a culture around the program's use.

Now let's investigate the incredible Photoshop 2024 tips and tricks.

The Preference Window

Photoshop has a ton of customization options. The software's settings, which govern many parts of Photoshop and allow you to turn features on or off, adjust how tools behave, and fine-tune how the program operates, let you make a lot of changes in addition to customizing the way its tools behave and how your workspace appears.

In Windows, you can find your **preference** in **Edit** the **Menu Bar** while in the macOS, choose **Photoshop> Preferences** to open the preferences dialog box.

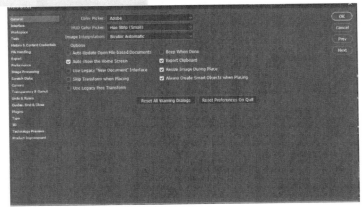

The Preference dialog window will be the platform upon which most of our tips and tricks will be taught.

To customize your Photoshop Interface do the following,

✦ After accessing your Preference dialog box, Click on **Interface** on the left side of the window dialog box and make the necessary changes.

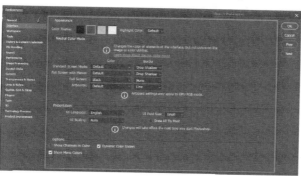

To change the ruler unit of measurement, do the following,

✦ Pixels, inches, centimeters, millimeters, points, picas, and percentages are just a few of the measurement units available in Photoshop. Before changing the unit of measurement, make sure the ruler is visible; if not, click **Ruler** on the **View menu** on the **Menu bar.**

✦ After the ruler displays at the top and left of your image, right-click anywhere on it to get a pop-up menu where you can choose the desired unit of measurement

Or

✦ From your Preference window dialog box, Select **Unit & Rulers.**

✦ Change your unit of measurement in the window that appears next.

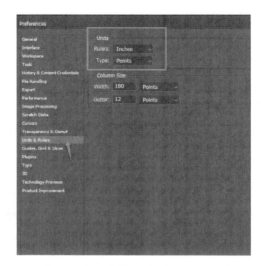

To change the appearance of your brush tips during usage, do the below,

⬍ After accessing your Preference settings, Click on **Cursor**
⬍ Make your modifications in the window that appears next.

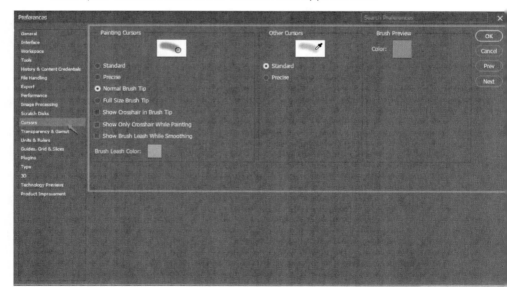

To search and find your required preferences, do the following,

⬍ To open the Preferences dialog, use **Cmd/Ctrl + K** on the keyboard.

- Now, use the Preferences dialog's search feature by pressing **Cmd/Ctrl + F** on your keyboard.
- Your result is the image below.

reference to improve Selection Stability

ue to NVidia Windows Display drivers, certain Photoshop desktop users on Windows ere encountering sluggish performance, crashes, or unforeseen selections. Changes ave been made to the app performance for Windows users who are experiencing these ifficulties. To improve the selection stability, follow the procedure below.

- To open the Preferences dialog, use **Cmd/Ctrl + K**
- Select **Image Processing** on the left side of the **Preferences dialog.**
- For Selections Processing, toggle from **Faster** to **More Stable**

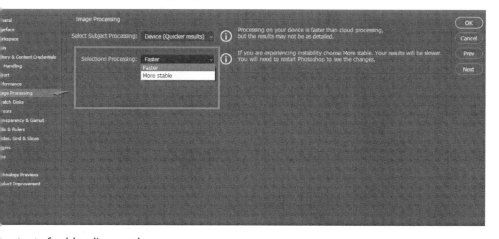

ortcuts for blending modes

hortcut Result	Windows	macOS
witch between blending nodes	Shift + + (plus) or – (minus)	Shift + + (plus) or – (minus)
o use the Normal mode	Shift + Alt + N	Shift + Option + N

To use the Dissolve mode	Shift + Alt + I	Shift + Option + I
To use the Behind Mode (brush tool only)	Shift + Alt + Q	Shift + Option + Q
To use the Clear Mode (Brush Tool Only)	Shift + Alt + R	Shift + Option + R
To use the Darken mode	Shift + Alt + K	Shift + Option + K
To use the Multiply mode	Shift + Alt + M	Shift + Option + M
To use the Color Burn mode	Shift + Alt + B	Shift + Option + B
To use the Linear Burn mode	Shift + Alt + A	Shift + Option + A
To use the Lighten mode	Shift + Alt + G	Shift + Option + G
To use the Screen mode	Shift + Alt + S	Shift + Option + S
To use the Color Dodge mode	Shift + Alt + D	Shift + Option + D
To use the Linear Dodge mode	Shift + Alt + W	Shift + Option + W
To use the Overlay mode	Shift + Alt + O	Shift + Option + O
To use the Soft Light mode	Shift + Alt + F	Shift + Option + F
To use the Hard Light mode	Shift + Alt + H	Shift + Option + H
To use the Vivid Light mode	Shift + Alt + V	Shift + Option + V
To use the Linear Light mode	Shift + Alt + J	Shift + Option + J
To use the Pin Light mode	Shift + Alt + Z	Shift + Option + Z
To use the Hard Mix mode	Shift + Alt + L	Shift + Option + L
To use the Difference mode	Shift + Alt + E	Shift + Option + E
To use the Exclusion mode	Shift + Alt + X	Shift + Option + X
To use the Hue mode	Shift + Alt + U	Shift + Option + U
To use the Saturation mode	Shift + Alt + T	Shift + Option + T
To use the Color mode	Shift + Alt + C	Shift + Option + C
To use the Luminosity mode	Shift + Alt + Y	Shift + Option + Y
To use the Desaturate mode	Sponge tool + Shift + Alt + D	Sponge tool + Shift + Alt + D
To use the Saturate mode	Sponge tool + Shift + Alt + S	Sponge tool + Shift + Option + S

To apply the Dodge/Burn Shadows	Dodge tool/Burn tool + Shift + Alt + S	Dodge tool/Burn tool + Shift + Option + S
To apply the Dodge/Burn Mid-tones	Dodge tool/Burn tool + Shift + Alt + M	Dodge tool/Burn tool + Shift + Option + M
To apply Dodge/Burn Highlights	Dodge tool/Burn tool + Shift + Alt + H	Dodge tool/Burn tool + Shift + Option + H

Saving Selections in Photoshop

To save yourself the stress of making a particular selection many times, saving the selection will be an easier way to ease yourself of such stress. Follow the instructions below to save selections in Photoshop.

✦ Make your selection.

✦ Select **Save Selection** from the **Select Menu** in the Menu Bar

✦ Name your selection then click **OK** to save your selection

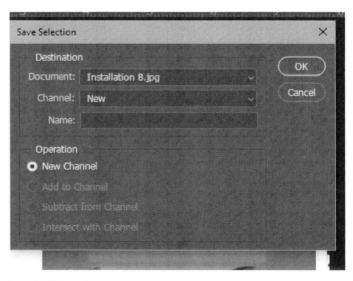

Loading Selections in Photoshop

Only saved selections can be loaded in Photoshop, Follow the instructions below to load your saved selections in Photoshop.

❖ From the **Select Menu** in the **Menu Bar**, Click on **Load Selection.**

❖ Select your saved selection and click **OK** to reopen it.

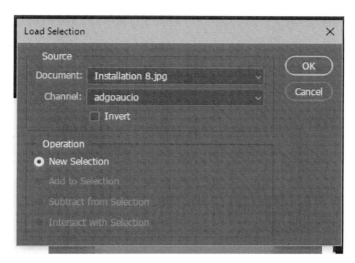

Popular Shortcuts in Photoshop

Shortcut Result	Windows	macOS
Free Transform	Control + T	Command + T
Toggle between painting and erasing with the same brush	Hold down~ (tilde accent)	Hold down~ (tilde accent)
Deselect Selections	Control + D	Command + D
Undo Last Command	Control + Z	Command + Z
Decrease Brush Size	[	[
Increase Brush Size	]	]
Decrease Brush Hardness	{	{
Increase Brush Hardness	}	}
Rotate the brush tip by 1 degree	Left Arrow (anti-clockwise), Right Arrow (clockwise)	Left Arrow (anti-clockwise), Right Arrow (clockwise)
Rotate the brush tip by 15 degrees	Shift + Left Arrow (anti-clockwise), Shift + Right Arrow (clockwise)	Shift + Left Arrow (anti-clockwise), Shift + Right Arrow (clockwise)
Default Foreground/Background	D	D
Switch Foreground/ Background	X	X
Fit layer(s) to screen	Alt-click layer	Option-click layer

Fit all to Screen	Alt + 0	Option + 0
New layer via copy	Control + J	Command + J
New layer via cut	Shift + Control + J	Shift + Command + J
Add to a selection	Any selection tool + Shift-drag	Any selection tool + Shift-drag
Delete Brush or Swatch	Alt-click brush or swatch	Option-click brush or swatch
With the Move tool chosen, turn on the auto-select checkbox in the Options bar.	Control-click	Command-click (Hold the Command key)
Close all open documents other than the current document	Ctrl + Alt + P	Command + Option + P
Cancel any modal dialog window (including the Start Workspace)	Escape	Escape
Choose the toolbar's first edit field.	Enter	Return
Move around the fields	Tab	Tab
Change the direction of your navigation between the fields.	Tab + Shift	Tab + Shift
Replacing Cancel with Reset	Alt	Option

Function Keys Shortcuts

Shortcut Result	Windows	macOS
Start Help	F1	Help Key
Undo/Redo		F1
Cut	F2	F2
Copy	F3	F3
Paste	F4	F4
Show/Hide Brush Panel	F5	F5
Show/Hide Color Panel	F6	F6
Show/Hide Layer panel	F7	F7
Show/Hide Info Panel	F8	F8
Show/Hide Actions Panel	F9	Option + F9
Revert	F12	F12

Fill	Shift + F5	Shift + F5
Feather Selection	Shift + F6	Shift + F6
Inverse Selection	Shift + F7	Shift + F7

Shortcuts for Selection Tools

Shortcuts Result	Window	macOS
Use the same shortcut key to switch between tools.	Shift-press shortcut key (if Use Shift Key for Tool Switch preference is selected)	Shift-press shortcut key (if Use Shift Key for Tool Switch preference is selected)
Go through all the hidden tools	Alt-click + tool (except Add Anchor Point, Delete Anchor Point, and Convert Point tools)	Option-click + tool (except Add Anchor Point, Delete Anchor Point, and Convert Point tools)
Move tool Artboard tool	V	V
Rectangular Marquee tool Elliptical Marquee tool	M	M
Lasso tool Polygonal Lasso tool Magnetic Lasso tool	L	L
Object Selection tool Quick Selection tool Magic Wand tool	W	W
Crop tool Perspective Crop tool Slice tool Slice Select tool	C	C
Eyedropper tool Color Sampler tool Ruler tool Note tool	I	I
Frame tool	K	K
Eyedropper tool 3D Material Eyedropper tool (ADD) Color Sampler tool Ruler tool Note tool	I	I

Count tool		
Spot Healing Brush tool	J	J
Healing Brush tool		
Patch tool		
Red Eye tool		
Content-Aware Move tool		
Red Eye tool		
Brush tool	B	B
Pencil tool		
Color Replacement tool		
Mixer Brush tool		
Clone Stamp tool	S	S
Pattern Stamp tool		
History Brush tool	Y	Y
Art History Brush tool		
Eraser tool	E	E
Background Eraser tool		
Magic Eraser tool		
Gradient tool	G	G
Paint Bucket tool		
3D Material Drop tool		
Dodge too	O	O
Burn tool		
Sponge tool		
Pen tool	P	P
Freeform Pen tool		
Curvature Pen tool		
Horizontal Type tool	T	T
Vertical Type tool		
Horizontal Type mask tool		
Vertical Type mask tool		
Path Selection tool	A	A
Direct Selection tool		
Rectangle tool	U	U
Ellipse tool		
Polygon tool		
Line tool		
Custom Shape tool		
Hand tool	H	H

Rotate View tool	R	R
Zoom tool	Z	Z
Liquify		
Toggle Standard/Quick Mask modes	Q	Q
Toggle Preserve Transparency	/	/
Previous Brush	,	,
Next Brush	.	.
First Brush	<	<
Last Brush	>	>

Shortcuts for viewing images

Shortcut Result	Windows	macOS
Go through open documents	Control + Tab	Command + Tab
Return to previous document	Shift + Control + Tab	Shift + Command + (grave accent)
Shut off a Photoshop file and launch Bridge.	Shift-Control-W	Shift-Command-W
Switch forward between Standard screen mode, Full-screen mode with menu bar, and Full-screen mode	F	F
Switch (back) between the following modes: Standard screen mode, Full-screen mode with menu bar, and Full-screen mode.	Shift + F	Shift + F
Forward-swiping canvas color	Spacebar + F (or right-click canvas background and select color)	Spacebar + F (or Control-click canvas background and select color)
Toggle the canvas's color backward.	Spacebar + Shift + F	Spacebar + Shift + F
Fit image in window	Double-click Hand tool	Double-click Hand tool
Magnify 100%	Double-click Zoom tool or Ctrl + 1	Double-click Zoom tool or Command + 1

Change to a hand tool (when not in text-edit mode)	Spacebar	Spacebar
Pan numerous documents at once with the Hand tool.	Shift-drag	Shift-drag
Switch to Zoom In tool	Control + spacebar	Command + spacebar
Use the Zoom Out tool now.	Alt + spacebar	Option + spacebar
Drag the Zoom tool while moving the Zoom marquee.	Spacebar-drag	Spacebar-drag
Keep the zoom percentage box open when applying the zoom percentage.	Shift + Enter to zoom in or out of the Navigator panel.	Use Shift + Return to zoom in or out of the Navigator panel.
Specified portion of an image is zoomed in	Control-drag the Navigator panel's preview.	Command-drag over the Navigator panel's preview
To Temporarily zoom into an image	Click the image while holding down the mouse button while holding down H.	Click the image while holding down the mouse button while holding down H.
Image scrolling using a hand tool	Drag the view area box in the Navigator panel using the spacebar.	Drag the view area box in the Navigator panel using the spacebar.
To Scroll up or down 1 screen	Page Up or Page Down	Page Up or Page Down
Scroll ten units up or down.	Page Down or Page Up with Shift	Page Down or Page Up with Shift
View can be moved to the upper-left or lower-right corner.	Home or End	Home or End
As Rubylith, toggle layer mask on and off (layer mask must be selected)	\ (backslash)	\ (backslash)

Shortcut for selecting and moving objects

Shortcut Result	Windows	macOS
Move the marquee while selecting	Any marquee tool + spacebar drag (apart from	Any marquee tool + spacebar drag (apart from

	single column and single row)	single column and single row)
Add to a selection	Any selection tool + Shift-drag	Any selection tool + Shift-drag
Take away from a selection	Any selection tool + Alt-drag	Any selection tool + Option-drag
Intersect a selection	Shift-Alt-Drag plus any selection tool (apart from the Quick Selection tool)	Shift-Option-drag plus any selection tool (apart from the Quick Selection tool)
Draw a marquee from the center (if no other selections are active)	Alt-drag	Option-drag
Change to the Lasso tool from the Magnetic Lasso tool	Alt-drag	Option-drag
Use the polygonal Lasso tool instead of the Magnetic Lasso tool.	Alt-click	Option-click
Widening/narrowing the detection window	Magnetic Lasso tool + [or]	Magnetic Lasso tool + [or]
Whether to accept cropping or not	Enter or Esc + Crop Tool	Crop tool + Backspace or Esc
Except when View > Snap is unchecked) Snap guide to ruler ticks	Shift-drag guide	Shift-drag guide
Change the direction of the horizontal or vertical guide	Alt-drag guide	Option-drag guide

Shortcuts for Selecting and editing texts

Shortcuts Result	Windows	macOS
Change the type in an image	When the Type layer is selected, control-drag type.	When the Type layer is selected, command-drag the type.
Choose 1 word left/right, 1 line down/up, or 1 character left/right.	Down Arrow/Up Arrow, Shift + Left/Right Arrow, or Control + Shift + Left/Right Arrow	Command + Shift + Left/Right Arrow or Down/Up Arrow, or Shift + Left/Right Arrow

Select characters from insertion point to the mouse click point	Shift-click	Shift-click
Move 1 word left/right, 1 line up/down, or 1 character left/right	Arrows to the left or right, up or down, or control while using the left or right arrows	Down/Up Arrows, Left/Right Arrows, or Command + Left/Right Arrows
To create a new text layer when a text layer is chosen in the Layers panel,	Shift-click	Shift-click
Choose a phrase, line, paragraph, or short tale.	Double-click, triple-click, four-click, five-click, etc.	Double-click, triple-click, four-click, five-click, etc.
show/hide the specified type's selection	Control + H	Command + H
When changing the bounding box's size, scale the text inside of it.	Control-drag a box handle to move it.	You may command-drag a bounding box handle.
To move the text box while creating a text box,	Spacebar-drag	Spacebar-drag

Troubleshooting in Photoshop

Without a doubt, one of Adobe's improved products with unique features included in Photoshop. But there will be one or two issues.

In this chapter's section, I'll focus on a variety of problems you could encounter and offer answers.

Issues	Solutions

Using the Select Subject or Object Selection Tool causes [Win] to crash. The Select and Mask and Object Selection tools are unavailable, and the Photoshop application crashes.	Use the official website to update your Nvidia drivers.
When you run Photoshop, it either freezes during setup or at the splash screen that reads "Loading Halide Bottlenecks..."	First, download the most recent version of Photoshop. If making the updates do not solve the problem then remove any large custom preset file.
To remove large custom preset files.	✦ Hold down the Option key when choosing Library from the Go menu in the Finder. Go to Preferences > Adobe Photoshop > Version Year > Settings. ✦ Look for the preset files with a significant file size in the Settings folder. Such preset files should be relocated from the Settings folder to a short-term location (for example, a new folder on your desktop).
When opening new documents, a green screen issue occurs. When you open a new blank document or an existing document in Photoshop 24.0, a green screen flickers in the background.	To get around this, take the following actions: ✦ Disable the Use Graphics Processor option under Preferences > Performance. ✦ restart Photoshop
Not recognizing the picture size copied to the clipboard The New Document dialog does not recognize the right image dimensions transferred to the clipboard when creating a new document with an image in it.	Check the Creative Cloud desktop app for updates. ✦ Click Check for Updates under the "Updates" tab in the Creative Cloud Desktop software. ✦ Try logging out and back into the Creative Cloud desktop app to see if that fixes the issue.
In the Save As dialog box, the Save button is inactive or non-responsive.	The Save button will become active once more if you slightly resize the save window.

After the macOS 12.3 update, Photoshop's Save As dialog box no longer has a working save button.	
Photoshop launches slowly (Win only) Photoshop may take a while to launch on your Windows machine.	Workaround: Take the following actions: ⬍ Your **Windows Image Acquisition** (WIA) settings need to be restarted ⬍ Change **Startup Type** from "**Automatic**" to "**Automatic (Delayed Start)**" in WIA attributes.
If you utilize Nvidia G-SYNC, Photoshop mouse stuttering may be an issue for you.	Take any of the following actions as a workaround: ⬍ Enter the Nvidia **Control Panel** > **3D Settings** > **Manage 3D Settings** to disable G-SYNC for Photoshop. Scroll down to **Monitor Technology**, choose **Fixed Refresh** from the dropdown option, and then click Apply after selecting Photoshop from the **Program Settings** tab. ⬍ Select **Technology Previews** > **Preferences** > and turn on **Deactivate Native Canvas**. Start Photoshop again.

Photoshop won't accept desktop photos from Lightroom Masks may need to be recalculated in Adobe Camera Raw when importing JPEG, HEIC, TIFF, PNG, and PSD files of pictures edited in Lightroom desktop to the Photoshop home screen. The masks may not always be found in their original shape.	If your Lightroom desktop photo masks cannot be recovered by Adobe Camera Raw, you can: • Lightroom exports images to your local machine. • Select Edit in Photoshop from the export option in Lightroom.

Photoshop unable to explore in Bridge
When you choose **File** > **Browse In Bridge** from within Photoshop, Bridge does not launch.
	Workaround: Take the following actions:
	• Remove Photoshop and Bridge from your computer.
	• Rename the following database folders:
	  o C:\Program Files (x86)\Common Files\Adobe\Adobe PCD
	  o C:\Program Files (x86)\Common Files\Adobe\caps
	• Install Bridge and Photoshop once more after removing them in Step 1.
	Using the Alt+Tab keys, you may also try switching from Photoshop to Bridge. On Mac ARM, though, this is not supported.

CONCLUSION

Well done on completing the Adobe Photoshop 2024 User's Guide. Now that you know the fundamentals of image editing, you can also apply some more sophisticated methods. You can now use Photoshop to start producing your own amazing pictures.

Here are some pointers to get you going.

Perfection comes from practice. Your proficiency with Photoshop will increase with usage. Make an effort to dedicate some time every day to honing your abilities.

Do a test. Take risks and try new things with Photoshop without fear. Enjoy yourself and see what you can come up with—there are no rules.

Employ resources. There are lots of resources out there to assist you in learning Photoshop. Books, webpages, tutorials, and even online courses are available.

Never give up. Although learning Photoshop can be difficult, it is well worth the effort. You will be able to use Photoshop to create incredible images with practice.

I hope you have found this book useful. Do not hesitate to get in touch with me if you have any queries or comments.

Have fun with your editing!

INDEX

3

3D Material Drop Tool   50

A

Adjustment Presets   iv, 4, 101, 102
Adjustments Panel   100
Adobe Photoshop   viii, 1, 5, 23, 30, 33, 77, 126, 150, 205, 231, 250, 279, 282, 283, 296, 329, 333
Artboard Tool   17, 42
Artistic Filter   vi, 303
Auto Color   iv, 28, 128, 132
Auto Contrast   iv, 28, 128, 130, 131
Auto Tone   iv, 28, 128, 131, 132
Auto-Commands   iv, 127

B

Bitmap Color Mode   iv, 81
Blending Mode   iv, 133, 134, 135, 136, 137, 138, 140, 141, 142
Blending Modes   iv, 87, 133, 135, 136, 137, 138, 140, 141
Blur Tool   250
Brush Tool   vi, 17, 46, 47, 48, 49, 170, 225, 228, 234, 237, 260, 261, 262, 274, 275, 279, 280, 281, 282, 283, 318

C

Camera Raw Filter   vi, 33, 295, 300
Character Panel   v, 30, 179, 183, 184, 193, 195, 196
Clone Stamp Tool   48, 225, 238
CMYK Color Mode   iv, 79
Color Modes   iv, 78
Color Replacement Tool   48, 225, 260
Color Sampler Tool   46
Content-Aware   v, vi, 47, 205, 209, 210, 211, 213, 216, 225, 226, 227, 233, 234, 235, 236, 324
Contextual Taskbar   iii, 22, 206
Crop and Slice Tools   44
Crop Tool   44, 213, 216, 218, 220

D

Drawing and Type Tools   51
Drawing Canvas   15
Duotone Color Mode   iv, 81

E

Edge Detection Settings   176
Elliptical Marquee Tool   43, 151
Eraser Tool   49
Eyedropper Tool   45

F

Filter Gallery   vi, 33, 294, 295, 298
Filters vi, vii, 33, 69, 293, 295, 296, 304, 305, 306, 307, 308, 309, 310, 311, 312, 313
Focus Area   v, 155, 162, 163, 164
Free Transform   v, 26, 198, 199, 201, 203, 321

G

Generative Fill   v, 2, 205, 206
Gradient Map   125, 126
Gradient Tool   49
Grayscale Color Mode   iv, 80

H

Healing Brush   vi, 46, 47, 225, 226, 227, 228, 229, 230, 231, 234, 235, 237, 250, 260, 324
Help   12, 16, 23, 38, 322
Home Screen   iii, 12, 59

I

Image layer   84
Image Retouching   v, 224
Indexed Color Mode   iv, 80

L

LAB Color Mode   iv, 80
Lasso Tool   43, 153, 171, 172
layer 2, 29, 31, 32, 36, 42, 47, 49, 50, 64, 66, 67, 68, 69, 70, 71, 72, 83, 84, 86, 87, 88, 89, 90, 91, 92, 93, 94, 95, 96, 97, 98, 99, 102, 107, 112, 116, 118, 120, 121, 124, 133, 134, 135, 136, 137, 139, 140, 141, 142, 143, 144, 145, 146, 147, 148, 149, 152, 155, 159, 164, 168, 177, 193, 194, 195, 196, 197, 201, 202, 203, 204, 211, 216, 226,

230, 233, 236, 238, 239, 241, 245, 248, 249, 250, 253, 256, 259, 260, 269, 270, 278, 286, 287, 288, 292, 293, 297, 299, 300, 322, 327, 328

Layer   iv, 12, 16, 23, 29, 67, 68, 69, 70, 83, 84, 85, 86, 88, 89, 90, 95, 98, 99, 112, 120, 121, 142, 143, 144, 146, 196, 197, 229, 239, 323

Layers   iv, 23, 37, 66, 67, 68, 69, 70, 72, 82, 83, 84, 85, 86, 87, 88, 89, 91, 92, 94, 95, 96, 97, 98, 99, 102, 113, 120, 123, 128, 133, 134, 143, 174, 175, 193, 194, 197, 233, 236, 244, 247, 249, 269, 288, 291, 293, 328

Lens Correction   vi, 294, 295, 301
Levels   103, 104, 300
Lightroom   iii, vii, 14, 15, 61, 63, 300, 332
Line Tool   54

M

Magic Eraser Tool   49
Magic Wand Tool   44, 49, 154, 160
Marquee Tool   42, 43, 151
Mask Options   v, 160, 168
Masking   v, 167, 168
Menu Bar iii, 16, 17, 23, 57, 71, 77, 99, 130, 131, 132, 144, 145, 155, 156, 157, 162, 201, 206, 207, 208, 273, 314, 319, 320
Move Tool   vi, 17, 42, 47, 225, 234
Multichannel Color Mode   iv, 81

N

Navigation Tools   54
Note Tool   46

O

Option Bar   17, 183, 220, 231, 233, 239

P

Paint Bucket Tool   50
Paragraph panel   v, 183, 190, 197
Parametric Filters   3
Pattern Stamp Brush   vi, 241, 242
Pattern Stamp Tool   48, 225
Photo Editing   224
Photo Enhancing   225
Photo Filter   28, 113, 115
Photo Retouching   224
Photoshop Tools   iii, 42
Place Embedded   iii, 64, 67, 68
Plugins   12, 16, 23, 37
Point Tool   51, 52
Preset Styles   iv, 145

Q

Quick Mask Mode   v, 164, 165, 166
Quick Selection Tool   44, 154, 169

R

Recent Command   iii, 63
Rectangular Marquee   42, 151, 323
Red Eye Tool   47
Reset Essentials   20
Retouching and Painting Tools   46
RGB Color Mode   iv, 79
Ruler Tool   46

S

Selection   iv, v, vii, 33, 36, 41, 42, 44, 53, 150, 151, 152, 154, 155, 156, 159, 168, 169, 170, 171, 174, 189, 202, 213, 233, 236, 317, 319, 320, 323, 325, 327, 329
Selective Color   124
Sharpen Tool   vi, 50, 225, 243, 250
Slice Select Tool   45, 213
Smart objects   iii, 70
Smart Objects   24, 29, 64, 65, 66, 67, 69, 70, 211, 293
Smudge Tool   vi, 50, 243, 250

T

Texts   v, 183, 192
The History Panel   vi, 280
The Marquee Tools   iv, 151
The Options Bar   173, 183, 229, 243
The Spot Healing Brush   v, 225, 226, 227, 231, 232
Tool iii, v, vi, vii, 3, 16, 17, 40, 42, 43, 44, 45, 46, 47, 48, 49, 50, 51, 52, 53, 54, 55, 56, 84, 151, 153, 155, 159, 163, 171, 172, 173, 183, 198, 207, 208, 213, 214, 216, 217, 218, 220, 225, 228, 231, 232, 233, 234, 235, 236, 237, 238, 239, 240, 241, 242, 243, 244, 245, 246, 247, 248, 249, 250, 251, 253, 254, 256, 257, 259, 260, 261, 265, 266, 269, 270, 273, 279, 281, 283, 286, 323, 328, 329
Tool Bar   iii, 40, 151, 155, 253, 254, 256, 259, 270
Tool Panel   16, 56
Transform   v, 26, 195, 197, 198, 199, 200, 201, 202, 204, 212, 235, 236, 297, 301
Troubleshooting   vii, 329
Typography   v, 179

W

Window   vii, 12, 16, 18, 23, 37, 85, 96, 100, 159, 168, 206, 280, 314, 323

Windows   iii, 1, 5, 6, 16, 19, 20, 21, 39, 41, 47, 55, 56, 57,
    62, 69, 92, 96, 121, 135, 136, 137, 138, 139, 140, 141,
    142, 145, 151, 152, 193, 194, 203, 204, 216, 217, 229,
    233, 239, 314, 317, 321, 322, 325, 327, 328, 330
Workspace iii, 12, 18, 20, 21, 38, 39, 55, 174, 178, 250, 322
Workspaces   iii, 15, 18

Z

Zoom Tool   55

Made in United States
North Haven, CT
10 May 2024

52367993R00183